MIND

Concepts and Principles

As Seen through Martial Arts

by

Barry B Barker M.A., L.Ac.

Crystal Pointe Media Inc., San Diego, CA

Mind: Concepts and Principles As Seen through Martial Arts

Barry B Barker, M.A., L.Ac.

Copyright © 2015

2021 4th Edition - Originally Published in 2015

Published by Crystal Pointe Media Inc.
San Diego, California

ISBN-13: 978-1540899828
ISBN-10: 1540899829

All rights reserved. No part of this book may be reproduced or transmitted in any form or by any means, electronic or mechanical, including photocopying, recording, or by any information storage and retrieval system, without permission in writing from the author at: BarryBBarker.com

DISCLAIMER

The contents of this publication are intended to be educational and informative. They are not to be considered a directive to use Martial Arts on other individuals. Before embarking on Martial Arts training, you should have clearance from your personal physician or health care provider then research and find competent instruction and training.

WARNING

This book and others in this series cover mature themes regarding Martial Arts techniques, targets and methods that can do serious and irrevocable harm to another human being. Its use is only made available for Self-Defense and Sport Fighting purposes and should never be misapplied.

Cover Design by Daniel Barnier

ACKNOWLEDGEMENTS

Thank you to GM Brian Adams for honoring me by reviewing my books and for writing the complimentary Foreword that I chose to place in this book on the Mind, Concepts and Principles.

To my longtime friend and classmate Tim Mullins for his review of many sections in this book and for being a great "dummy" (i.e., training partner), thank you Tim.

Thanks also to my Black Belt students Daniel Barnier for his graphics work, plus Cassie Li, Patty Alvarez, and Jennifer Nila for their proofreading skills in this book.

I appreciate and thank you all.

To my Black Belt sons, Josh and Jordan, thank you for demonstrating your expertise in many of the video links and always giving me quality feedback. Seeing you grow in skill and maturity gives me unexplainable joy and makes me proud of the men you have become.

Barry B Barker, M.A., L.Ac.

DEDICATION

Family

My passion for martial arts could not have been fulfilled to the degree it has if it were not for my family. Not enough can be said about the stability family brings to a man's life.

To my kids, thank you Justin and Alexis for understanding why I missed so many functions when you were young because I was always at the studio, thanks Joshua and Jessica for being the nucleus of our incredible kid's program back in the day, and thank you Jordan for just being awesome. I love you all and am so proud of my incredibly talented children and thank you Rosie for the support you gave me for so many years.

Me with my 5 Kids Thanksgiving 2014
L-R: Justin, Jordan, Me, Josh, Alexis, Jessica

My school's 30-Year Anniversary Party October 2014 with my then 83-year old mom

This book, and the entire series, is dedicated to my mom who raised my two sisters and me, and who gave me the gift of confidence. She had her two favorite sayings for me as an undersized young boy who attended 7 different elementary schools, some in bad neighborhoods.

Whenever I was feeling like the "little guy," she would tell me one or both of them. "Remember Barry, it's not the size of the dog in the fight, it's the size of the fight in the dog" and "The bigger they are, the harder they fall."

Thanks mom for believing in me, and for always being my biggest fan.

PREFACE

This is one of a three book series I gave myself as an advanced Black Belt thesis project, and for the personal growth I expected would accompany the effort. Another big project of mine was attaining a Master's Degree in Chinese Medicine and subsequent Acupuncture Licensing. Rank integrity is important, so I am compelled to make a large effort towards that end. This I hope sets a good example for my children and my students.

These books are not only a reference resource for practitioners of my American Kenpo style but where martial art enthusiasts in general can benefit from the many non-style related chapters in the series, such as *Concepts & Principles, Pressure Points, Sport Fighting,* and *Martial Arts First Aid*. Any athlete can benefit from the discussions on *Breathing, Balance,* and *Exercise & Nutrition*, and even curious observers may find *Qi* and *Yin/Yang* theory interesting.

My 3-book series is formatted using one of the oldest and most accepted martial art concepts traditionally sought for development, the *Mind, Body,* and *Spirit*. This is the book of the *Mind*.

My personal biography is at the back of this book but suffice to say that my formal training began in 1973, just not seriously until 1980. I opened my Kenpo Karate School in 1984, which has been my full-time job for over 30 years as of my books original writing, and I added a sport fighting gym in 1998. These experiences have given me the background to write about the subjects covered in this and my other books.

During this time, I have been able to put my entire system on video so anyone interested can watch and study my Kenpo system. All of my videos are at BarryBBarker.com where they are accessible on any computer or mobile device. I also have a YouTube Channel where searching Poway Martial Arts will get you to mostly Demos and Events from my longtime school in Poway California.

Also, throughout my books there are, often colorful, Kenpo technique names in parenthesis to reference a visual of what is being discussed. Note: The technique names I use are different than the IKKA/EPAK names of the Ed Parker American Kenpo System, although the original techniques came from that system. It's a long story explained more fully in Chapter II.

The use of empty-handed martial arts can be divided into the four main training intentions of *Military, Law Enforcement, Civilian Self-Defense,* and *Sport Fighting,* with definite crossover value between and within those approaches. Weapon arts and movement arts are not covered in my books, necessarily.

In summary, the *Military* objective is to attack and kill the enemy. *Law Enforcement* (bouncers included) train to subdue the "bad guy." The *Civilian Self-Defense* objective is not to fight yet be prepared against criminal assault or if in an interpersonal conflict. The training goal of *Sport Fighting* is to win a competition within the rules and guidelines of the sport.

The *Mind* is utilized for each of these martial intentions with my books primarily coming from the *Civilian Self-Defense* and *Sport Fighting* perspectives.

This book on the *Mind* contains *Vocabulary and Terminology* along with *Concepts and Principles* chapters, much of which transcends all martial art intentions. *Anatomy, Physiology, Pressure Points,* and the *Martial Art System* are covered extensively in the book of the *Body*, with *Tradition, Wisdom,* and other intangibles covered in my book of the *Spirit*. Information, insight, and perspective from my Chinese medical background will be offered where useful and appropriate.

My observation is that we are all on a knowledge and wisdom continuum relative to each other. A knowledgeable reader may agree, disagree, or know more about a particular subject, but my hope is that a martial artist approaches every learning opportunity with an empty cup hoping to gain from the experience.

The contradiction with attaining knowledge and wisdom is that if we think we know everything then that is all we will know, where if we think we know nothing then knowledge is always flowing in our direction. My advice is to let others judge where you are on the continuum and keep approaching each day humble, as if you know nothing.

For myself personally, my children, and my students is the expectation to be always striving for knowledge. I have noticed in myself that I have never stopped learning over my entire life so there is no reason for me to think it will stop with this book project. I humbly submit this work as what I know now. After all, time may be eternal, but knowledge and wisdom are relative.

FOREWORD
By Grand Master Brian Adams

In 1967 I presented my manuscript "The Medical Implications of Karate Blows" to Ed Parker. Mr. Parker immediately saw it as setting the standard for the first IKKA Black Belt thesis requirement, creating the precedence for future members to strive for. I am happy to see that this tradition has continued to thrive in the Kenpo community.

I have read a manuscript [Mind-Body-Spirit] by Mr. Barry Barker L.Ac., AMA, Kenpo 8th Degree Black Belt and Chief Instructor at Poway Martial Arts. Regarding the work, in the words of my instructor Ed Parker, "I was more than overjoyed that this thesis was informative enough to be published and I echo my support of this massive work."

Mr. Barker's Pressure Point chapter [Body] especially shines as a much sought-after light on the complexities of a martial aspect fantasized by many. My interest in the legendary Dim Mak lore from China can now be explained as an academic off shoot of Chinese medicine. No great mystery, just the science of the East.

The other books [Mind and Spirit] are also very thorough in covering their respective subjects. They are a cross between "The Art of War" and "The Tao of Jeet Kune Do." This work could easily be entitled "The Encyclopedia of The Art and Science of Kenpo" and will be a much sought-after text for all serious martial artists. As a one of a kind it will become a classic work, and I loved the chapter on "Wisdom" [Spirit], especially the quote from 'Sitting Bull."

Grand Master of Integrated Martial Arts
Brian Adams

MIND

TABLE OF CONTENTS

I.	**THE MIND**	1-3
II.	**VOCABULARY AND TERMINOLOGY**	4-36
III.	**MENTAL CONCEPTS**	37-104
	Motivation	38-39
	Intention	40-43
	Yin/Yang	44-46
	Qi/Chi/Ki	47-48
	Breath	49-56
	Planning: O-S-T	57-61
	Posture	62-64
	Balance	65-72
	Focus	73-74
	Speed	75-76
	Power	77
	Directions & Angles	78-81
	Distance & Timing	82-86
	Dimensions & Zones	87-96
	Contouring	97-98
	Targets	99
	Weapons	100
	Equation Formula	101-103
	Levels of Force	104
IV.	**PHYSICAL PRINCIPLES**	105-151
	Motion & Movement	106-122
	Muscle/Movement Preload	123-126
	Muscular Acceleration	127
	Whipping Acceleration	128
	Springloading	129
	Wave Transference	130
	Torque & Rotation	131-132
	Dropping/Settling	133
	Lifting/Rising	134
	Collapsing/Compressing	135
	Expanding	136
	Rebounding	137
	Stretch Reflex Acceleration	138
	Major/Minor Principle	139-140
	Mechanical Advantage	141-146
	Borrowed Force	147
	Voluntary Momentum	148
	Manipulated Voluntary Momentum	149
	Involuntary Momentum	150-151
BIBLIOGRAPHY		**152**
ABOUT THE AUTHOR		**153-154**

THE MIND

Chapter 1

Enlightened Mind    **Intentional Mind**

Mind-Body-Spirit as an integrated whole is a common thread that transcends martial art styles and practitioners. It is used and referenced regularly in the teaching and practice of martial arts worldwide. Every developed field however has mental understanding, physical technique, and developmental aspects.

Although appearing straightforward, Mind-Body-Spirit can be interpreted differently by the human mind. A martial art teacher or organization can see a different order of importance, place more emphasis on one component, or have another interpretation. The reality is that although analyzed separately they are developed simultaneously.

In holistic health circles, Mind-Body-Spirit is a related and integral part of the healing process. Overlapping this, Traditional Chinese Medicine (TCM) describes "Three Treasures" or essential energies for sustaining human life, the "Jing" or nutritive refined essence, the "Qi/Chi" or vital energy, and the "Shen" or soul.

The *Mind* is where interest or curiosity starts so without it there is no inquiry or effort. The mind also must gain a basic understanding before the body can begin to attain the wisdom in technique while building muscle memory; then spirit, effort, enthusiasm, and passion can be infused.

The *Body* is concerned with the application of physical technique, the 'what' and 'how' and 'where' of using weapons and targets. The different perspectives, or styles of martial arts, can vary in emphasis depending on its purpose. The terminology and approach here reflect my Kenpo style but since as humans we are all the same species then any martial art based upon sound principles can be of benefit to an individual.

The *Spirit* provides the motivation to train leading to an enthusiasm to continue. The spirit also drives the execution of martial art technique by providing the fire in movement and the desire behind purpose. Spirit also refers to development by providing structure, etiquette, discipline, and the wisdom that make learning martial arts about more than just fighting.

Eastern medicine for thousands of years views the heart as where thoughts, memory, and intellect reside. The physical brain is the prevalent wisdom in the West. Both would seem to have merit as the physical brain is needed for storage but must have blood pumped from the heart for thoughts to be accessed and felt through the body and be acted upon.

TCM also makes the diagnostic observation that long-term memory is stored in the heart, with short-term memory stored in the kidneys, also blood-filled. An acupuncturist could use this in determining a treatment protocol for a patient with loss of memory as a symptom.

These can be broken down into more refined concepts as the calm mind is termed differently than the mind stirred or engaged by thought. *Mind*, *Body*, and *Spirit* each have these multiple aspects represented in the Chinese symbols that start each chapter I in this book series.

The mind works best when challenged, maintained, improved upon, and allowed to rest and recover. This is done through study and practice of things that interest us, while we are hopefully enjoying life. This learning process should be ongoing as it strengthens and improves our minds.

Discipline is required to keep learning, especially when we are old enough to decide for our self or after having some personal accomplishments, and maybe gaining some status and recognition in life.

It is also important that we put good things into our *mind* and avoid things that can corrupt or poison it. Just as we would not intentionally bring an illness into our physical body, we should try to avoid bringing toxins into our minds whether substances, thoughts, or images. This is where the *spirit* can and should lead the *mind*.

The same way parents try to filter what their children see, and experience, teens and adults should make this same effort to keep toxic elements from invading the *mind*. We must also forgive ourselves for mistakes we make in life while allowing our minds to heal from the emotional scars that are an inevitable result of living.

Keep good thoughts and see the good, keep the glass half full while trying to eliminate bad and negative thoughts. Remember past lessons while living in the present and looking positively towards the future. These are keys to keeping the *mind* healthy.

This book refers to the minds engaged intellectual knowledge and understanding of martial arts with my base style of Kenpo as a point of reference, but much of what is covered are universal to all martial arts and other physical disciplines.

Formulating solutions in the human mind begins with how we see and adapt to our environment. This process starts with an *Idea* that leads to *Theory* that leads to experimentation which then evolves into *Concepts* and *Principles* to find answers. We then teach others so a continuous line of improvement can be made. These reference pillars apply to any martial art system, style, or movement discipline that has a lexicon. With that as a baseline this book is written with the *Mind* in mind.

IDEA

An *idea* is an imagined thought, usually perpetuated out of some need in our lives. The need for survival in ancient and modern times has contributed to the idea that we need methods to protect ourselves.

Developing our physical body, using environmental props, or evolving specialty weapons have obviously led to discoveries that could be refined. These would have led to theories about what is and was useful to various peoples all over the world at various times in history. This would have stimulated the observation of concepts to develop those theories that could be proven and developed using universal principles.

THEORY
The *theories* that stemmed from the idea of self-protection must have run the gamut, and still do. Some theories can be proven with principles and real-life experience while others fall short of real value. Nevertheless, theories abound, especially in martial arts.

Many are universally accepted such as having the knees bent for athletic movement from the feet to occur. Others are at odds with each other such as the fist rotation preferences between, for example, the vertical fist punch of one style and the horizontal fist punch of another, with other styles like Kenpo searching for the value in both applications.

Some theories are useful to some but not to others, like a "fighter" who thinks training in form movement is a waste of time or a "forms stylist" who thinks that fighters are missing important movement lessons and the art in martial arts. There are also those who see the value in both, the yin/yang balance of refined movement with useful application.

CONCEPT
A *concept* is part of a refinement process the brain uses when developing an *idea* and/or expanding a *theory*, and then links them with the principles needed to accomplish it. Once the idea is envisioned and theories of how to implement it are expressed the *concepts* are the nuances that support the effectiveness proven by *principles*.

PRINCIPLE
Not to be confused with the school "principal" as I often need to clarify with younger students, the *principles* here refer to basic provable truths that need no explanation in the real world, although perhaps in the academic world where truth can often be relative.

Gravity for example is a basic truth. An apple will fall to the ground when it separates from its stem on a tree. Sir Isaac Newton is credited with noticing it, conceptualizing about it, and defining the terms surrounding the phenomenon, but the truth is that apples had been falling from trees long before Newton "discovered gravity."

Another definition of the word principle is as a moral standing, a rule or belief that governs someone's personal behavior. This is also an important subject but for another context. The definition here will relate to the fundamental truth about the application and practice of martial art technique.

VOCABULARY AND TERMINOLOGY
Chapter 11

Many of the terms listed in this chapter had their martial art origins with American Kenpo founder and Grandmaster Edmund K Parker (1931-1990). He developed, formulated, and collected an extensive vocabulary and terminology list during his lifetime that he put into his 5 "Infinite Insights into Kenpo" book series and subsequent "Encyclopedia of Kenpo." Mr. Parker literally wrote the books on American Kenpo, so I would also recommend those books for anyone interested in Kenpo.

Throughout my books Kenpo Self-Defense Technique names are listed, usually in parentheses, as examples. These use my AKA (American Kenpo Alliance) names. When my instructor at the time, Jim Mitchell, left the IKKA in 1984 he moved away from the EPAK (Ed Parker American Kenpo) names which use a coded naming system (i.e. hair = feathers, twigs = arms, etc.).

See the conversion chart in the *Body* Self-Defense Technique chapter for Mr. Parker's IKKA and related Tracy Kenpo names, and thanks to my Black Belt student Dr. John Hippen for organizing that list.

Many of Mr. Parker's terms are used here but I have added to, rewritten, differentiated, and left out terms that didn't apply to the focus of this book. Some descriptions are also organized here under one heading to show their relationship to other terms (e.g. *Stages of Learning* under one heading rather than three).

Some terms and concepts originally from Mr. Parker are verbatim and in quotes with many I have expanded upon after his description or in other parts of this and my other books. There are also many new terms that I have added.

Many slang terms and specific *Basics* from Mr. Parker's collection are not included here as they are irrelevant to this book and individual basics are covered extensively in my book on the *Body*.

A martial art system like any discipline has a lexicon. Mr. Parker developed, organized, and expanded the Kenpo and martial art lexicon for all to have. My hope is to add where appropriate, reorganize where needed, clarify where lacking, and pare down where cumbersome.

One of my book project goals is to contribute to refining the essential elements of the martial arts lexicon by contributing to its organization. I hope you enjoy my efforts and can gain benefit from it.

Alphabetically:

ACCELERATION – An increasing change in speed or velocity over time, generally in a direction, of which there are two types.

1) To move faster or gain speed/velocity through the path of a straight or linear motion, like an accelerated punch.

2) To move faster or gain speed through the path of a circular motion, i.e. revolutions per minute. This can result in a circle getting smaller towards its center, dramatically increasing its speed upon impact (Snapping Arm); or for the circle to get larger causing an increase in speed that culminates in a whipping energy at its apex (Triggered Palm). See *Angular Momentum*.

For martial art purposes, *acceleration* is more than just a component of physical speeds raw acceleration of a mass creating force ($F=ma$) that over a distance (time) becomes power, the beneficiary of acceleration.

Between human beings the effective point of acceleration happens as a weapon reaches then impacts a target. Getting there involves timing changes in acceleration to create and follow openings with angular & circular adjustments allowing for less travel time that increase perceived acceleration, along with the intentional will to accelerate.

ACCEPTANCE – The first of Ed Parkers *Preparatory Considerations*. It refers to the recognition, mental reality, awareness, and acknowledgement of possible danger, and a need for action.

ACTION-REACTION – Related to "Newton's Laws of Motion" that when one body exerts force onto another that second body exerts equal force in the opposite direction, "every action has an equal and opposite reaction." In martial arts this also refers to the timing that anticipates or uses an opponent's reaction against them.

ADD – When another movement is put into a technique sequence as analyzed by the "Equation Formula." This can be done at the beginning to prefix, as an insert in the middle, or at the end to suffix a sequence.

ADJUST – Changing, modifying, adapting an application to be more effective and relevant. One of the 8 "Equation Formula" ingredients/options.

AFFECT – An action that is caused to occur. See *Effect* to differentiate.

AGITATOR ACTION – The back and forth motion (like in a washing machine) utilized in many Kenpo techniques (Broken Kneel).

ALIGNMENT – "The precise adjustment of our torso and limbs so that they are arranged in direct line with each other for the purpose of utilizing total body mass."

ALIGNMENT OF MUSCULAR FORCE – Ways in which the physical structure of the arms and legs are positioned and how those can be moved to generate force by pushing or pulling, and the sub-categories within those. See *Physical Principles* chapter, Pg 115.

ALTER – One option contained within the *Equation Formula*. In this context it refers to varying a weapon and/or target within a prearranged self-defense technique sequence. See *Mental Concepts* chapter, Pg 102.

ANALOGY - A figure of speech, often used in teaching, relating the idea of one subject with that of another. Describing something familiar with similar aspects to something less familiar does this.

Describing an upward elbow strike motion is similar to answering the telephone, or an inward elbow to looking at a wristwatch, or a more complex analogy relating movement to a written language. See *Metaphor* and *Synonym* to differentiate.

ANATOMY – The study of the human body by its parts and organized by systems within the entire organism. For martial arts use this can be narrowed down to structures that can be seen with unaided vision, with understanding internal structural locations also beneficial. See *Physiology* to differentiate and *Anatomy & Physiology* chapter in the *Body*.

ANATOMICAL POSITIONING – Controlling an opponent's relative position and posture by striking, angular checking, controlling, or using our own posture in a way that makes them vulnerable to a strike or maneuver.

Kicking an opponent in the groin causes him to bend forward moving his face closer to a strike (Thrusting Palm), or an offline step to help avoid a roundhouse kick (Bouncing Pendulum).

ANATOMICAL BODY REFERENCES – Terms used that more precisely describe body reference points, relative position, location, and direction. They are:

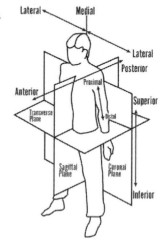

Transverse Plane - Top/Bottom halves
Sagittal Plane - Left/Right sides
Coronal Plane - Front/Back halves
Anterior - Front
Posterior - Rear
Superior - Above
Inferior - Below
Lateral - Towards the outside
Medial - Towards the middle
Proximal - Nearer the body
Distal - Further from the body

ANCHOR – "To weigh down the elbow or buttocks for better leverage, coverage, or control." The buttock weighs down, so the hips and lower torso settle on top of the legs, with the elbows down so the shoulders and upper torso settle. Done together they make for an even stronger anchor.

AND – "A word in our Kenpo vocabulary that is eliminated by the more adept. It involves time and therefore is contradictory to economy of motion – a principle well worth following."

This original definition refers to employing one or more wasted counts, pauses, hesitations, or cocking a motion between strikes. This is for efficient movement in the *Ideal Phase,* but timing breaks and hesitations are a natural part of adjusting within unplanned unrehearsed fight sequences. This makes it not 'always' eliminated by the more adept but used. See *With & Then* to differentiate and *Broken Rhythm*.

ANGLES – In mathematics there are three components to an angle. The *vertex* is the corner point of an angle. The *arms* are the two straight sides that stem from the *vertex*, and the *angle* is the gap between the *arms* and the *vertex*. Together they make up six distinct types of angles.

Part of the martial art analysis of human physical interaction and body positioning for attack and defense recognizes and uses these shapes. Angles are everywhere in nature and a useful evaluative tool a martial artist can use to help improve the efficiency and effectiveness of fighting technique. See *Mental Concepts* chapter, Pg 79.

ANGLE OF CANCELLATION – "A controlled angle, which places an opponent in a precarious position, thus minimizing or even nullifying the use of his weapons."

This is neutralizing an opponent's options through *Body Alignment* and *Anatomical Positioning*. This body position cancellation can be done by direct aggressive force against an attacking weapon, slight angle deflections, adjusted body alignment, or any combination of those. Note: *Angle of Deflection* is part of the *Angle of Cancellation*.

ANGLE OF CONTACT – Any angle used to apply a weapon onto a target for maximum effectiveness. This can be a 90° angle but could also be a glancing or slicing angle that redirects off a target after impact. See *Angle of Incidence* to differentiate.

ANGLE OF DEFLECTION – Moving the attacking weapon by blocking, parrying, or jamming to create a change in that weapons path. This is the difference between the intended path and the adjusted path. Note: *Angle of Deflection* may or may not result in an *Angle of Cancellation*.

ANGLE OF DELIVERY – "The position from which one's natural weapons may be executed with accuracy, efficiency, and effectiveness." The efficient path a motion travels from *Point of Origin* to *Point of Destination*.

ANGLE OF DEPARTURE – Exiting to the safest most efficient direction.

ANGLE OF DEVIATION / ADJUSTMENT – Angular movements, usually done with the feet, to a safer zone of defense; and/or positioning for a stronger offensive alignment.

ANGLE OF DISTURBANCE – "That angle created when a move is executed that does not necessarily injure but rather upsets an opponent's balance." Or changes his direction and/or affects his posture.

ANGLE OF ENTRY – "Any degree, or path (angle) of approach, whether linear or circular in execution, that allows you or your opponent access to specific targets. The path of approach can be executed horizontally, diagonally, or vertically from any direction."

Finding the most efficient path to a target is the shortest distance between two points. This is not necessarily a straight line, but the most direct path. See *Line of Entry* to differentiate.

ANGLE OF INCIDENCE – "The 90° angle formed when a weapon strikes a target." See *Angle of Contact* to differentiate.

ANGLE OF NO RETURN – The position or rotation of the upper body and hips to where it becomes awkward, not practical, or advisable to try and return to along the same path, aka "point of no return."

The classic Kenpo example is done in the self-defense technique *Buckling the Leg* where after rotating the hips, dropping the weight, and extending a side thrust kick, it would be difficult and unnecessary to readjust the hips back to the *point of origin,* so a front crossover step is done to exit.

ANGLE OF OBSCURITY – Blind spots, or positions outside peripheral sight, of which there are two perspectives known in Kenpo as *Zones of Obscurity* or *Obscure Zones*.

The first is from the hitter's viewpoint where weapons are positioned in such a way as to occupy an opponent's blind spots, or utilized from an existing position to take advantage of blind angles, e.g., under the chin, behind the ears, the spine, etc. The second is awareness of our own blind spots which can provide us an opportunity to move, realign, or check those angles.

ANGLE OF PROTECTION – "The positioning of your body to give you maximum shield against anticipated strikes."

ANGLE OF REDIRECTION – The degree of change made or used after a slicing or glancing strike.

ANGULAR MOMENTUM – The amount of rotation an object has around a center point, considering its mass and shape. This can be a fixed distance around, like a ceiling fan or a spinning leg sweep. It can also increase/decrease in distance from the center like how a figure skater pulls their arms in to spin faster and opens them to slow down, or the footwork into a spinning outward hook kick. See *Acceleration*.

APPLICATION – The physical practice of martial art movements on another person(s). Various levels of contact in training help us know how different people will attack and react to movement, and how delivering different movements affect our own body. This is where concepts and principles are tested, and where physical endurance is developed. See *Theory* to differentiate.

ARC – Any curved line that is part of a circle. See *Circles*.

ATTACH – Movements supported within our own body structure and/or interlocked with an opponent. See Motion & Movement Pg 120.

AWARENESS – The intention to observe, which in the martial arts context is used in many ways from conceptual to spatial, mental to visual, instinctive to trained, etc.

BACK-UP MASS – "The use of body weight that is directly behind the action that is taking place." Using one body part aligned behind another like an elbow behind a fist to punch, or for support like finger knuckles stacked to form a handsword. This relies on *body alignment* at the point of contact, and a term often interpreted to include the entire body mass behind an application.

BACK STOP – Using our body or an inanimate structure to support part or all of an opponent's body to increase the potential for compression. Pressure can then be effectively applied as in a step over armbar (Pinch from Death C), knee bar (Straddling the Leg), or smaller wristlocks (Thrusting Blade). See *Bracing, Weld, Compression*.

BAD POSITION DRILL – A training drill where at least one person is setup to begin from an undesirable starting point. For example, starting with someone behind or with a submission hold in place while grappling, or working out of the corner in stand-up fighting/Boxing.

BALANCE – The position, posture, and alignment of a static or active body that allows for body control relative to gravity or to a supporting structure. See *Counterbalance* to differentiate and *Mental Concepts* chapter, Pg 65.

BASE POSITION – A balanced and controlled neutral posture where attacking or defending movements can begin, and a place to return to if/when an attack attempt is unsuccessful. It is a place to start from or regroup to that exists in stand up striking, clinch, and ground fighting.

BASICS – Individual martial art movements categorized by method. These include *stances, foot maneuvers, blocks, parries, checks, punches & strikes, kicks, holds & locks,* and other *specialized moves*. See 'Body' *Basics* chapter.

BLACK DOT FOCUS – A black dot on a white background showing total awareness. Differentiate with *White Dot Focus* and see *Mental Concepts*, Pg 73.

BLOCKING – Any method used to intercept an attacking weapon with perpendicular contact to stop or redirect it from the intended target. This can be done with the arms, legs, or other durable body parts.

Karate styles typically teach aggressive blocking maneuvers that use a striking motion against an attack where boxers and sport strikers tend to catch and use the shoulders to absorb punches with kickboxers adding legs to block low kicks.

BODY ALIGNMENT – "This is the coordination of body parts in order to harmonize their angles of travel so that they all move together, in line, and in one direction. This principle, when followed, automatically triggers the principle of *Back-Up Mass*."

BODY FULCRUM – "The natural curvatures of the body used as a launching platform to add leverage, bracing, or acceleration to the speed and force of any weapon." See *Contouring*.

BODY FUSION – "A concept in which body parts move as a unit prior to relaying action to other parts of the body." A downward block or an inward heel-of-palm strike both move from the shoulder with a slightly bent elbow statically locked in place.

BODY MANEUVERS – A category of basics that involves moving the torso of the body with evasive or setup action while standing as done in Boxing with riding, turning, rolling, slipping, bobbing, and weaving movements along with leaps, jumps, and all the types of falls and rolls. See *Basics* chapter in the *Body*.

BODY MECHANICS – "The technical utilization of the body in the science of motion and action, that allows the forces therein to be fully maximized. In short, highly technical knowledge of the proper use of the body in reaching or obtaining maximum results."

BODY MOMENTUM – One of Ed Parkers key concepts closely aligned with *Back-Up Mass, Body Alignment,* and *Directional Harmony,* but discussed and differentiated here under *Inertia* and *Momentum*. It uses the weight and bulk of the body through accelerated height, width, and depth zones to add support to the penetration directly behind punches, strikes, kicks, and takedowns.

BORROWED FORCE – Using an opponent's force against him. See *Physical Principles* chapter, Pg 147.

BRACING – Using a part of <u>our body</u> to support a part of an <u>opponent's body</u>. Holding an opponent's head down with the palm while doing a rear scoop kick thru their face (Sweeping the Leg) or holding their chin up with a forearm to expose the throat to a half-fist strike (Pursuing Panther). Differentiate with *Bracing Angle*.

Contributing movement variables can be connected line to line, circle to circle, line to circle, or circle to line. Rebounding directional change variables are either off a target or off our self in a strike succession. Range variables move towards or away from an opponent using footwork and/or limb length to reach a target, including the hand extending after an elbow strike (Hooking Arms) or elbow folding onto a target after hand contact (Triggered Palm). See also *Sequential Flow, Kinetic Chain, Wave Transference,* and the *Physical Principles* chapter.

COMPRESSING / COMPRESSION – The result of two forces meeting or collapsing together around or on either side of a common structure attempting to diminish the size of that structure with pushing, squeezing, and/or striking pressure. See *Back Stop, Sandwiching, and Physical Principles chapter,* Pg 135.

CONCEPT – A universally true, but often abstract human notion such as time, or the human creation of numbers and letters that allow for other mental frameworks like mathematics and language to exist.

CONNECT – The feel on a target or body surface after initial surface contact. See Motion & Movement Pg 119.

CONTACT – When two objects physically interact or collide. In martial arts this has a wide range of uses from touching to various degrees of impact.

CONTENT – The information or the 'what' about a subject or position. Lifting the knee in front is a mechanical body motion that can be done for multiple reasons, or for no reason. See *Context* to differentiate.

CONTEXT – The intention, purpose, or the 'how' something fits or is evaluated and used to accomplish an objective. Lifting the knee to hit and/or then extending the foot to kick someone's groin or punt a football are reasons for this mechanical motion.

CONTOURING – Following the natural curves and lines of the body. Methods are body contact for striking; body contact for checking; and non-body contact methods. See *Mental Concepts* chapter, Pg 97.

CONTRACT – To move away from, make smaller, diminish, or reduce in range, and is what muscles do when flexed.

CONTROL – "The regulation of force to produce (a) accuracy as well as (b) the degree of injury."

The intention to not injure when: 1) Practicing with training partners; 2) Preventing an opponent's actions by checking; 3) Directing an opponent with compliance techniques.

COORDINATION – Using the body as a complex unit in a controlled and directed manner with balance and proprioception awareness so the moving parts work together efficiently and effectively to perform a physical activity.

COUNTERBALANCE – Using one's weight or force to influence, offset, or check an opposing force. Seen in the natural gait of human movement where one shoulder moves directionally with the opposite hip. This motion is often exaggerated to apply martial arts technique and is especially noticeable when kicking. See *Balance* to differentiate.

CROSSED EXTENSOR REFLEX – The involuntary response to excessive limb stimulation or injury that follows the *Touch Reflex* as it withdraws from pain. As the limb in danger is withdrawn the opposite side limb is engaged (crossed extensor) in the opposite direction. See *Touch Reflex* to differentiate.

The standard example is stepping on a tack causing that foot to retract quickly, i.e. *Touch Reflex*, as the opposite foot plants onto the floor, i.e. *Crossed-Extensor Reflex*, absorbing the body weight, or if one arm is stimulated to retract the opposite arm instinctively goes forward.

DAN / TAN TIEN – A Chinese martial art and Traditional Chinese Medicine (TCM) term referring to the body center. It resides inside the body between the navel and the pubic bone in men and inside the uterus in women. This is the root of balance, Qi, breath, power, and health.

DEFANGING THE SNAKE – A term, attributed to Filipino martial arts, that refers to injuring an opponent's attacking body part. This often involves damaging the hand or arm holding a knife or other weapon but can also refer to a punching hand or arm or kicking leg or foot.

DIMENSIONS – Three ways of measuring: height, width, depth (or length).

DIMENSIONAL STAGES OF ACTION – "The viewing of the space or gap between you and an opponent from all aspects of height, width, depth, and direction, with regard to the distances that are necessary in maintaining, closing, controlling, and opening the gap. Each view or stage logically requires long, medium, and close-range techniques while closing in on an opponent, or when covering out."

DIMENSIONS & ZONES – The collection of *Zones of Protection* or *Zones of Attack or Defense* used to analyze height, width, and depth dimensions separately, three-dimensionally as in the *Quadrant Zone Concept* and *Six-Gates Theory*, from the eye's perspective as *Obscure Zones*, and spatially as *Zones of Sanctuary*. See *Mental Concepts* chapter, Pg 87.

DIRECTIONAL HARMONY – "Having all of your action moving in the same direction."

DYNAMIC STRUCTURAL ALIGNMENT – Correct body alignment transitioning from one position to another with posture and a properly aligned musculoskeletal structure to optimize leverage, backup mass, and acceleration. See *Kinetic Chain*.

ECONOMY OF MOTION – "Entails choosing the best available weapon for the best available angle, to insure reaching the best available target in the least amount of time while still obtaining the desired result." Efficient movement travels from *Point of Origin* to *Point of Destination* by following the most direct path, not necessarily a straight line as used in martial arts.

EFFECT – The result of an action. See *Affect* to differentiate.

ELLIPSE – An oval with two center focus points that connect at different lengths to a third point making for increased acceleration moving into or out of the smaller segment. See *Circles* to differentiate.

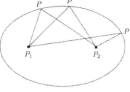

ENERGY – The ability to perform *Work* by virtue of its *Force*. See *Potential Energy* and *Kinetic Energy* to differentiate.

ENERGY, KINETIC – The energy associated with motion. See *Potential Energy* to differentiate.

ENERGY, POTENTIAL – The energy built into a preloaded body structure or position that when/if released explodes outward. A basic fighting stance with bent knees and hands up is full of this energy waiting to be used, where it then becomes *Kinetic Energy*.

ENVIRONMENT – "It is everything around you, on you, and in you at the time of confrontation."

ENVIRONMENTAL AWARENESS – "The ability to observe daily conditions and surroundings and make on the spot decisions to either avoid danger or take advantage of opportunities offered."

This is GM Parker's second *Preparatory Consideration* of self-defense where it refers to seeing the physical surrounding and assessing potential danger to speed up development of strategies for defense and escape.

EQUATION FORMULA – Developed by Ed Parker, it allows for flexibility in a *Self-Defense Technique* to assess the "what ifs" *(Phases of Learning)*. See Pg 101.

The 8 formula traits for a standard Kenpo Self-Defense Technique are:
<u>Prefix</u> – Adding a move before the first move in the sequence
<u>Suffix</u> – Adding a move after the last move in the sequence
<u>Insert</u> – Adding a move between two other moves in the sequence
<u>Delete</u> – Take a move out of the sequence
<u>Rearrange</u> – Change the order of two or more moves in the sequence
<u>Alter</u> – Changing a weapon and/or target in the sequence
<u>Regulate</u> – Changing the emphasis and/or timing of one or more moves
<u>Adjust</u> – Changing your or an opponent's body alignment using the feet, torso, or physically affecting the opponent's position

EXPLOSIVENESS – A characteristic of martial art movement, and Kenpo movement specifically, that involves going from stillness to maximum speed instantly. A Kenpo analogy is that dynamite does not gradually explode but happens in a sudden violent destructive burst.

EXTENSION – Increasing the angle between two joints like the elbow joint opening to move the hand away from the shoulder. See *Flexion* to differentiate. This term also refers to the expanded version of Kenpo base Self-Defense Techniques.

FAKE – Changing our position or timing to cause an opponent to change their position or posture. A distraction or false lead in which a weapon or body part is twitched, flinched, or moved to cause a reaction from an opponent, followed by a committed action. *Broken Rhythm* is a common type of fake but in general terms it is any physical, verbal, or psychological attempt to fool or trick. See *Feint* to differentiate.

FAMIILY GROUPINGS – "Movements that stem from the same source, position, point of origin, or point of reference. Although these moves stem from the same point of origin, their methods of execution vary according to circumstance."

This crosses over into methods of organizing Kenpo system Self-Defense Techniques as designed by GM Parker and is built into his *Web of Knowledge*, with its 9 types of attack.

These 9 are further broken down into 18 *Family Groupings* categorized as *Wrist Grabs, Shoulder/Lapel Grabs, Hair Grabs, Belt Grabs, Tackles, Pushes, Punches, Kicks, Hand Holds, Full Nelson Holds, Bear Hugs, Chokes, Locks, Gun, Knife, Stick, One-Man Multiple Attack* and *Two-Man Multiple Attack.* Pulling is noticeably missing from this list but could be inferred into Shoulder/Lapel Grabs.

Other groupings can be conceptualized by *Range, Angle of Attack,* or relative lower and upper body standing base positions divided into four *Closed Stance* (L-L or R-R) and four *Open Stance* (L-R or R-L) postures. See *Self-Defense Technique* chapter in the *Body*.

FEEL – "A word used to describe the foot or hand as it slides from one point to another." Moving with the feet continuously connected to the ground helps maintain balance and leverage to maneuver efficiently with adjustment flexibly on smooth environments, or around obstacles. Kenpo movement is observed as if skating on the ground with good posture, head level, and feet connected, yet light.

Another use of this term is the hand(s) *Sliding* or *Tracking* along an opponent's body. It is used for checking and to help find targets, and in the case of *Frictional Pull* acts to break balance.

FEINT – Changing <u>our</u> body position to attack an <u>existing</u> opening and/or method to draw attention in a way that leaves an open target vulnerable to attack. See *Fake* to differentiate.

FLEXION – Decreasing the angle between two joints, like the elbow joint flexing to bring the hand toward the shoulder. See *Extension* to differentiate.

FOCUS – "Is the result of the entire body working as a unit at the very instant a target is struck. The concentration of mind (knowledge), breath, strength, and methods of execution must unite as one in conjunction with body momentum, torque, gravitational marriage, timing, speed, penetration, etc. It must be remembered that it is not just the concentration of weapon meeting target, but the entire body meeting the target as one unit that fully defines the term FOCUS."

FOOT MANEUVERS – A *Basics* category referring to various ways of moving the feet to close and create distance or change direction. Distance changing maneuvers are divided into *Half-Step, Full-Step,* and *Two-Step* maneuvers, with three in-place positional change maneuvers. See *Basics* chapter in the *Body*.

FORCE – The capacity to do *Work* or cause physical change; the energy, strength, or active power exerted on an object causing it to move; Physics measures this in "pound-force" or "Newton's," defined as "the influence on a body or system that produces or tends to produce a change," with the math equation: "the magnitude of force is equal to the product of body mass and its acceleration ($F=ma$)." See *Power* to differentiate.

FORCE COUPLE – Moving or rotating more than one load around a middle point. See *Mechanical Advantage* section, Pg 145.

FORM – A pattern of often pre-arranged choreographed martial movements done *in-the-air* utilizing combined basics. These help to develop body posture, alignment, and symmetry of movement while indexing the techniques of a system, or themed around a common martial goal, or done as freestyle movement. Also known as "Kata" (Japanese), "Poomsae / Hyung" (Korean), and includes "Shadow Boxing" from Western sport fighting. See *Set* to differentiate.

Other benefits include physical conditioning, mental programming, muscle memory development, directional awareness, improved transitions, solo training, etc. See the *Sets & Forms* chapter in the *Body*.

FORMULA – A set of Principles expressed as a rule to relate a Concept that supplies the framework for analyzing the variables of a subject.

FORMULATE – "Combining of moves into a systematized order" that "develops into a logical and practical sequential arrangement."

FRAMING – Building a structure with the musculoskeletal system that surrounds another surface for the purposes of controlling and/or damaging.

FRICTIONAL PULL – "A method of pulling and unbalancing an opponent with the use of friction," "caused by attaching then sliding, scraping, hooking and pulling." Sliding our forearm along an opponent's forearm(s) from their elbow(s) to their wrist(s) to clear the arms, break balance, and affect posture by drawing their weight forward and down.

GAP – "The existing distance between, or that separates, you and your opponent." The space between combatants. See *Range* to differentiate.

GAUGING DISTANCE – "The ability to systematically regulate the distance between an opponent and our self for purposes of defense or attack." Movements practiced *in-the-air* do not require the same degree or adjustment variables as is necessary when moving with a live person.

GEOMETRIC SYMBOL CONCEPT – "The use of circles, squares, triangles, etc. as a visual and mental training aid while learning the angles and paths one must take," when defending or attacking. The forearm, from hand to elbow, of an inward block traces a square or perhaps rectangle as the arm moves through space. All motions can be visualized following geometric paths.

GOLGI TENDON ORGAN (GTO) REFLEX – The neurological mechanism within a muscle structure located in a muscle tendon. Its purpose is to protect the tendon from tearing if bearing too much weight by causing an involuntary muscle relaxation, therefore stimulating this GTO also causes the associated muscle to relax. See *Muscle Spindle Cell* (MSC) to differentiate and the *Pressure Point* chapter in the *Body*.

GRAFTING – The blending or borrowing of movements from one, or more than one, pre-arranged technique sequence based upon changing circumstances. See *Equation Formula*.

GRAVITY – The relentless force that attracts a body toward the earth. In martial arts this phenomenon makes it necessary to feel a balanced center (dantien) with structural integrity while moving and applying leverage. This is done while trying to disrupt those same qualities in an opponent.

GUIDELINING – "A contact method of Contouring where an entire surface area is used to guide your natural weapon to its target...it follows a path of action." See *Tracking* to differentiate.

HEALTH MATRIX – The group of considerations used to help determine someone's fitness goals, exercise routines, workout regimen, and activity related interests. These include constitution, body type, overall health, available time, talent, interest, and goals of training. See health related chapters in the *Spirit*.

HIDDEN MOVES – Movements that are not obvious within a path or position of motion but are applied with a purposeful intention. These can attack additional targets within the flow of a movement or can originate in obscure zones where they cannot be seen by an opponent.

HOLDS – Using the hands and/or arms to surround a part, or more than one part, of an opponent's anatomy by checking, controlling, submitting, or injuring to immobilize, make uncomfortable, or to cause pain.

IMPACT – Penetrating movements, however applied, that explode onto and perhaps into a target surface. See *Motion & Movement*, Pg 119.

INERTIA – The tendency of the body, whether still or in motion, to remain still or in motion until another force interferes with its path, i.e. Newton's first law of motion.

This is seen in martial arts as the force that leads or is in front of the mass. The punching knuckles, although the body is behind them, contains the inertia that will penetrate, slow down, stop, or be redirected upon contacting a target. See *Momentum* to differentiate.

INTENTION / INTENTIONAL MOVES – Any effort that is done on purpose towards accomplishing a goal or task. See *Unintentional* to differentiate.

JAMMING – The intercepting, attacking, or interrupting of an action before it fully accelerates. This is done best at the source or root of a strike, kick, or tackle, but can be successful further along the path if the attacking weapon is disrupted before its focused contact point.

KENPO FLOW – A continuous flow of integrated, bilateral, gaseous, spherical motion strategically applied for maximum protection with the possibility of maximum destruction, devastation, and/or annihilation.

KEYLOCK – A method of cinching a hold to maximize applied leverage by interlocking the hands and arms in a way that becomes more structurally sound and progressively tighter, while becoming more difficult to defend, counter, and affect a release.

KIAI (Kee-aye) – A Japanese language term that refers to the yell of the spirit that focuses the "Ki," or Qi in Chinese. The sound that emanates is not necessarily the phonetic name "Kee-aye," but any method that verbally expresses the compressed release of the internal pressure of the breath while applying force.

KICK – Methods of striking involving the legs and feet that includes sweeps, buckles, stomps, and striking using the knees, shins, and various parts of the feet, including the ball, instep, heel bottom, back, knife-edge, and toes. See *Basics* chapter in the *Body*.

KINETIC CHAIN – A term used in sports medicine to describe the connectivity of mind, nerves, muscles, bones, and attachments by the body to perform physical activities and respond to stimulus. See *Wave Transference,* Pg 125.

LANGUAGE OF MOTION – An analogy that relates the English language with the movements of Kenpo. Originally coined and described by the late Kenpo Master Ed Parker. See *Motion & Movement,* Pg 106. Note: My explanation is slightly different than Mr. Parkers.

LEVEL – Maintaining the same head and body height while moving with good posture as the feet *Feel* the floor observed as skating/sliding along the ground. Not moving up or down keeps power and flow of action moving in the same direction and is practiced with footwork and stance drills. Rising or dropping is acceptable however when power is needed in those directions.

Another meaning uses this term to assign a degree of knowledge and skill level to a practitioner (e.g. Beginner, Intermediate, Advanced, Expert, etc.).

LEVERAGE – Any method of force that uses a *Fulcrum* with an applied *Effort* to move a specific *Load*. A useful acronym to help remember the components of a lever is E.L.F. for Effort – Load – Fulcrum, which can be arranged in 3 distinct ways. See *Mechanical Advantage,* Pg 143.

LINE – The straight direct path between two points.

LINEAR MOVES – Movements that travel along a straight direct path or line from *Point of Origin* to *Point of Destination*.

LINE OF ATTACK – The seeing of target openings from the weapons perspective. See *Point of Origin* and *Line of Sight* to differentiate and the *Sport Fighting* chapter in the *Body*.

LINE OF DEPARTURE – "The line, angle, or direction combatants can move to when escaping that will place them in a secure position." It is the preferred or best available exit angle direction away that minimizes an opponent's response and/or to avoid other opponents.

LINE OF ENTRY – "That line or path of penetration that allows you or your opponent access to targets." In standup fighting, this is determined by the front foot position relative to an opponent's front foot. This could be inside, outside, in front of, or on top of that foot. See *Angle of Entry* to differentiate.

LINE OF SIGHT – The seeing of target openings from the eye's perspective. See *Line of Attack* to differentiate.

LOWER CASE MOVEMENT – Using lower body weapons or sections of the body to attack or defend. See *Upper Case* to differentiate.

MAJOR EFFECT – The result of any movement causing a mechanical or tissue function disruption such as a joint dislocation, bone break or eye injury, along with moves that cause unconsciousness, disability, or death. See *Levels of Force* Pg 139 and the *Pressure Point* chapter in the *Body*.

MAJOR MOVES – Attacking movements that can cause immediate devastation to the target and/or opponent. These are generally hard-hitting movements with maximum body weight with acceleration and leverage applied using heavy force with serious intent to do bodily harm. See *Physical Principles* chapter, Pg 139.

MANIPULATE/MANIPULATION – Moves that force an opponent into a position or posture they otherwise would not place themselves making them vulnerable to follow-ups, cancelling their ability to apply technique, or placing them as an obstruction to another opponent. Methods include pushing, pulling, twisting, locking, holding, checking, and striking.

Ed Parker defined three types:
CONTACT MANIPULATION: "The orchestration of control, once contact is made, to contour, leverage, takedown, restrain, twist, sprain, lock, dislocate, choke, etc., to increase the effectiveness of an action."

CONTROL MANIPULATION: "To sustain control of your opponent's actions while steering or maneuvering" them "to a more suitable and strategic positions. Setting up these positions not only helps to prevent further retaliation but allows you clear access to your opponent's targets as well."

COUNTER MANIPULATION: "1) The stage of motion that is utilized just prior to employing the principle of opposing forces to its maximum;" "2) Turning or twirling in the opposite direction from a previous twirling move."

MARRIAGE OF GRAVITY – The settling of body weight and mass while applying a natural weapon. There are four ways of executing this principle. See *Dropping/Settling* Pg 133.

MASTER KEY MOTION(S) – Anatomical motions with multiple application potential. The arm for example can circle inside or outside, "wax on wax off," with vectors isolated to apply intentional movement. A Form like Kenpo's Short Form 1 indexes the inside circle at the inward and outside downward blocking/vector positions, with the outside circle indexed at the outward, upward, and inside downward blocking/vector positions. Differentiate with *Master Key Movement(s)*.

MASTER KEY MOVEMENT(S) – "A move or series of moves that can be used in more than one predicament. For example, a rear heel kick, shin scrape, and instep stomp can be used for a Full Nelson, Rear Bear Hug with the arms free or pinned, Rear Arm Lock, etc. Similarly, an arm break can be applied to a cross wrist grab, a lapel grab, or hair grabs – application of the arm break would remain constant, but the methods of controlling the wrist would vary."

MATHEMATICAL SYMBOL CONCEPT – Using the +, -, and x symbols to analyze directions and paths of travel. It is often used in conjunction with the *Clock Concept* but can also imply adding, subtracting, and multiplying in the context of martial art movement and intention.

MATTER, 4 States of – Solid, liquid, gas, and plasma, with the first three traditionally used in Kenpo as an analogy to distinguish between types and levels of movement. The fourth level of plasma, e.g. fire, lightening, etc., is added to that analogy as the explosion that happens when a weapon impacts a target. See *Physical Principles* chapter, Pg 121.

<u>Solid Motion</u> - Seeks/maintains its stature
<u>Liquid Motion</u> - Seeks its level
<u>Gaseous Motion</u> - Seeks its volume
<u>Plasma State</u> - Electrically charged energy current

MECHANICAL – Beginning stage of learning. See *Stages of Learning*.

MECHANICAL ADVANTAGE – An engineering term that covers *Leverage*, *Wedge*, and *Force Couple*. See *Physical Principles* chapter, Pg 141.

METAPHOR – A figure of speech often used in teaching in which a term is transferred from one object to another by implied comparison. Example: They hit like a truck, or move like the wind, or are fast as lightening, etc. Sometimes called a simile with the term metaphor is used here. See *Analogy* and *Synonym* to differentiate.

MINOR EFFECT – A movement that gets an attacker's attention, controls, causes discomfort, strain, or sprain. See *Levels of Force,* Pg 139.

MINOR MOVES – Attacking movements that are not heavily applied and may even be glancing in nature. The name is deceptive because these moves can also cause great harm, such as any eye poke or an ear box. These "minor movements" could cause a *Major Effect*. See *Physical Principles* chapter, Pg 139.

MOMENTUM – The residual motion behind a mass seen in martial arts as an accelerated weapons penetration until slowed by target resistance. This is Newton's second law of motion described as the "impetus or force gained through movement as a product of a body's mass and linear velocity," where "Momentum P = Mass x Velocity." See *Inertia* to differentiate.

MOTION – A continuous flow of energetic movement from one place to another through open space. See *Physical Principles* chapter, Pg 106.

MOTION, ANGLES OF – The route or course an object travels or can travel horizontally, vertically, and diagonally. See *Physical Principles* chapter, Pg 105.

MOTION, DIMENSIONS OF – The spatial relationship of an object, or what lies between multiple objects as measured by scale and magnitude using height, width, and depth. See *Physical Principles* chapter, Pg 110.

MOTION, DIRECTIONS OF – The vector that an object travels or can travel through going forward, backward, sideways, inward, outward, upward, and/or downward. See *Physical Principles* chapter, Pg 110.

MOTION, METHODS OF MECHANICAL – The function and ranges of motion the muscles and joints of the arms and legs can perform. These are the unique individual mechanical movements of the arms and legs. See *Physical Principles* chapter, Pg 110.

MOTION, PATHS OF – The *Linear* or *Circular* path a moving object covers travelling too or through an object. See *Physical Principles* chapter, Pg 110.

MOVEMENT – The refined mechanics of human kinetic motion as used to accomplish a task. See *Physical Principles* chapter, Pg 109.

MOVEMENT, KNOWLEDGE OF – The basics, patterns, and technique information a martial arts practitioner knows. See *Level of Movement* to differentiate.

MOVEMENT, LEVEL OF – The skill, coordination, posture, balance, alignment, and effectiveness with which a martial arts practitioner moves and applies his knowledge. See *Knowledge of Movement* to differentiate.

MOVEMENT / MOTION KENPO – The flow of Kenpo movement in the air or along the body surface often used in training where circular and linear motions can connect with efficient footwork, timing, and dynamic flow, but without the adjustments or damage created by contact.

This term is sometimes directed in a derogatory way towards those who it is thought only know this method without the ability to apply and adapt onto a physical body as the application of Kenpo technique can and should dramatically influence an opponent's anatomy on many levels.

MOVEMENT (MUSCLE) PRE-LOAD – The potential energy stored in a contracted or readied muscle before it is applied. See *Physical Principles* chapter, Pg 123.

MUSCLE SPINDLE CELL (MSC) REFLEX – The neurological mechanism within a muscle structure located at the motor point in the muscle belly also known as the "stretch reflex" that causes a muscle contraction if struck. See *Golgi Tendon Organ (GTO) Reflex* to differentiate and the *Pressure Point* Chapter in the *Body*.

MUSCLE-TENDON ELASTICITY – See *Stretch Reflex Acceleration*

MUSCULAR ALIGNMENT – Placing the body's musculoskeletal structure in proper order for maximum leverage and effect.

NUCLEAR WEAPONS of KENPO (i.e. going Nuclear) – Last resort use of certain weapons to specific targets with the intention to obliterate. These include attacking the throat/neck, spine, eyes, ears, and other vital areas. Having "nukes" in an arsenal adds to overall confidence and preparedness for a worst-case scenario.

NEWTONS 3 LAWS OF MOTION:
Universal principles of motion published in 1686 by Sir Isaac Newton, born in England on Christmas Day in 1642, died at age 85 in 1727.

1. "Every body continues in its state of rest, or of uniform motion in a straight line unless it is compelled to change that directional state by forces impressed upon it." In people, this is greatly influenced by the intention to move and apply movement.

2. "The change of motion is proportional to the motive force impressed and inversely proportional to the mass and is made in the direction of the right line in which that force is impressed." This is the "boards don't hit back" rebuttal, as they actually do hit back, according to Newton.

3. "To every action there is an opposed equal reaction: or, the mutual actions of two bodies upon each other are always equal and directed to contrary parts." This action-reaction law is where both happen simultaneously and is also greatly influenced by intention in martial arts, along with size of the board and the type of wood (that's a metaphor).

OBJECTIVE – Your goal or what you expect to accomplish. It usually involves a plan of action with varying degrees of determination to attain. This is also a component of *Intention*. See *Mental Concepts* chapter, Pg 57.

OFF-ANGLE – Moving the feet in such a way as to change body alignment towards an opponent.

OPPOSING FORCES – The converging of two forces, increasing the impact of a collision.

OPPOSING STRUCTURAL MOVEMENTS – Manipulating another body structure to cause control and/or cause damage, i.e. moving the chin to one side while moving the shoulders to the other (Jumping Crane).

OPPOSITE – The other side of the body or mirror image. The opposite of right is left, etc. See *Reverse Motion* to differentiate.

ORBITAL CHANGE – Changing to a different orbit at the end of circular strike. An inward hammerfist to the temple traveling across on a 3-9 line that upon hitting the solid temple changes direction into a forward elbow on a 12-6 line (Shielding Fingers).

ORBITAL ADJUSTMENT – "A slight degree of change when altering the orbit of your action." This alignment change to a circular strike is based upon target realignment or alternate selection so a hammerfist intending to hit the nose can be changed in flight to hit the collarbone.

OUTER RIM CONCEPT – "An imaginary egg-shaped circle that is used as a visual aid", this "egg-shaped pattern starts at eyebrow level, and ends slightly below the region of the groin", "this concept teaches you to confine defensive and offensive movements of your arms and hands to those areas within the imaginary circle."

PARRYING – A defensive method used to intercept an opponent's attacking weapon by matching and riding it past the intended target with the major difference from blocking being the angle of contact. This allows a weapons momentum to continue forward yet miss its intended target, making an attacker more vulnerable to a counter. See *Blocking* to differentiate and the *Basics* chapter in the *Body*.

PATH TO DESTINATION – The line or arc that a weapon travels through from *Point of Origin* to *Point of Destination*. The shortest distance between two points is not always a straight line so term refers to the most direct path.

PENDULUM – "A term used in self-defense techniques referring to a downward block or strike." A Pendulum is a free swinging weight suspended from a pivot point so this can also refer to body parts that hinge off a joint such as the upper arm at the shoulder (elbow strikes), lower arm at the elbow (hammerfist strikes), upper leg at the hip (knee kicks), and lower leg at the knee (hook kicks).

PENETRATION – "This involves depth of focus. It is the extension of power beyond the selected target to insure the desired force and to compensate for the distance to be traveled."

PERSPECTIVE – This describes an outlook or as something is seen and interpreted. In fighting this can mean not only seeing with the eyes but also yours or an opponent's potential weapons, as they have their own perspective regarding entry angles to possible targets.

PHASES OF LEARNING – "The analytical process of dissecting a technique."

IDEAL PHASE (Phase I): Formulating fixed moves of defense against defined attacks with anticipated reactions. Kicking someone in the groin causing them to bend forward is an anticipated reaction in the design of many Kenpo techniques.

WHAT-IF PHASE (Phase II): Taking the anticipated reactions from the *Ideal Phase* and projecting other possible reactions. We kick him in the groin but miss and hit his hip causing him to turn.

FORMULATION PHASE (Phase III): Where adjustments are made instantly and continually in a free-flowing live environment considering anticipated and alternative reactions then making necessary adjustments to achieve success. We want to kick him in the groin, but the angle is closed off, so we kick his knee instead.

PHYSIOLOGY – The study of how human body parts function. See *Anatomy* to differentiate and *Anatomy & Physiology* chapter in the *Body*.

PIVOTING – Methods of turning while on a connected surface. Foot pivot points are mainly heel or ball with several combination variables. The hand can also pivot on an opponent's body to adjust, control, or cause damage.

PLYOMETRICS – A type of exercise designed to improve explosive movement by loading a muscle then contracting it repeatedly in a rapid sequence. This develops explosive muscular power by challenging muscular strength and the fast twitch muscle fibers. See *Exercise Basics* in the *Spirit*.

POINT OF CONTACT – "Location of impact where weapon meets target."

POINT OF CONTACT VARIABLES – Methods of applying force at the *Point of Contact* with the 3 major categories of *Impact, Connect,* and *Attach,* all with sub-categories. See *Physical Principles* chapter, Pg 119.

IMPACT: The acceleration of body projectiles intended to explode onto or into a selected target(s). These penetrate body tissue to break, crush, smash, knockout, takedown, tackle, or puncture. Associated terms include striking, punching, kicking, hitting, slapping, poking, bumping, tackling, pushing, shoving, etc.

CONNECT: Surface level body contact for transitioning, monitoring, controlling, affecting posture or position, and/or damaging surface tissue. Associated terms include sliding, pressing, vibrating, checking, pinning, rubbing, scraping, gouging, sticking, tracking, raking, touching, feeling, etc.

ATTACH: Wrapping the hands, arms, or legs around a body part either individually, interlocked with our own structure, or with an opponent's, to hold, manipulate, cause pain, or submission. Associated terms include grasping, grabbing, grappling, locking, stretching, twisting, holding, pinching, squeezing, pulling, etc.

POINT OF DESTINATION – The end or completion site of any movement. See *Point of Origin* to differentiate.

POINT OF ORIGIN – "The beginning, root, or source of any movement." See *Point of Destination* to differentiate.

POSITIONING – Three physical locations relative to our environment:
1) Standing vertical with no obstruction (no barrier)
2) Standing against a wall or object (vertical barrier)
3) Lying on the ground (horizontal barrier)

See *Family Groupings* for positioning relative to opponent/training partner.

POST – A grappling term that describes a bracing maneuver, often on the ground, to keep our foot, hand, or other body part from moving, e.g. fence post.

POWER – The amount of time it takes to affect a target with a weapon. In physics, it is the rate at which *Work* is done or transmitted using *Energy*, mechanically measured in *Horsepower*, with the formula as energy dispersed over time. See *Force* to differentiate and Pg 77.

PRACTICE – Going through learned moves and routines at different speeds from slow to fast or with applied effort from soft to hard but rehearsing to primarily reinforce knowledge and muscle memory with fitness as a side benefit. See *Training* to differentiate.

PRE-STEP – A foot adjustment before an intended maneuver. It can be intentional to change a body angle, adjust a joints position, pre-load for more power, used as a fake, and/or as a timing break. It can also be unintentional or observed in an untrained, or under trained, opponent with poor mechanics that telegraph their intended move(s).

PREPARATORY CONSIDERATIONS – "The initial planning of logical preventive measures to avoid danger or eliminate a physical encounter from occurring." Pg 55.

In my opinion, one of Ed Parkers most brilliant observations, with #1 and #2 especially important for self-defense and street art practitioners. From his book 1, chapter 11 in order of importance as listed by him: 1) Acceptance; 2) Environmental Awareness; 3) Range; 4) Position; 5) Maneuvers; 6) Targets; 7) Natural Weapons; 8) Natural Defenses

PRESSURE POINT – The term used to describe sensitive areas on the body that when stimulated with various techniques can result in healing or any of the 7 *Levels of Force* with a martial arts intention. The six areas affected are Blood, Air, Nerves, Brain, Mechanical Ability, and Qi. See *Pressure Point* chapter in the *Body*.

PRINCIPLE – A basic truth or law of the universe, i.e. a universal truth. It can also be an assumption or belief that can be used as a rule of action to prove and explain the working aspects of a Concept.

PROACTIVE REACTION – To anticipate an opponent's attack by observing their posture or set them up with an opening it is anticipated they would attack and that we are prepared to counter. This is the essence of counter-fighting.

PRY – Using the lever action of a moving wedge to progressively force open increasing space between objects. See *Type 1 Lever* Pg 143.

PUNCH – A closed fist striking method applied with the third pharyngeal joint (knuckles) of the middle and index fingers that has 270° of hand rotation and used to configure with a target upon accelerated impact. Methods for folding the fingers into a tight fist are:

1) little finger then ring, middle and index; 2) index first then middle, ring and little; 3) middle finger first with others following. In all cases, the thumb then overlaps the second phalange of the index and middle fingers perpendicularly to hold the folded fingers in place.

Punching weapons with a sharper edge use the second pharyngeal joint extended to use a single index or middle knuckle or all the fingers as a half-fist or knocking punch with the thumb shifted for structural support.

RANGE - The distance weapons must travel to reach targets. See *Distance and Timing* and *Gap* to differentiate.

RANGE OF MOTION (ROM) – The number of degrees a joint can move from a flexed to an extended position. A straight arm hanging to the side can swing back about 45° or be lifted forward and up overhead about 180°. Depending on the activity and muscular stability there is a trade off with having more or less ROM in a joint.

RANGE DEPTH ZONES FOR SELF-DEFENSE – The distance(s) between combatants broken down into 5 primary ranges. They are *Out-of-Range, In-Range, Contact Range, Penetration Range,* and *Manipulation Range*. See *Physical Principles* chapter, Pg 82.

RANGE DEPTH ZONES FOR SPORT FIGHTING – Methods of engagement used in sport martial arts. Encompassed and included in self-defense ranges but from the viewpoint of a "fair fight" between two willing combatants using striking, clinch or stand-up grappling, and ground grappling. See *Physical Principles* chapter, Pg 83.

REGULATE – Controlling the timing, tempo, force, and intention of an actions. One of the 8 "Equation Formula" ingredients/options, Pg 102.

REFLEX REACTION – The natural and uncontrollable human response to defend and repel sudden excessive stimulation. This occurs without mental thought through the nervous system to withdraw from the threat. Individual senses have their own unique responses.

The visual response is the blink reflex, auditory is a duck reflex, an overpowering smell causes a sour face reflex, a disgusting taste causes a spitting reflex, something deep in the throat causes a gag reflex, and a painful or unwanted touch causes a withdrawal reflex.

Especially useful in martial arts are the *Golgi Tendon Organ Reflex (GTO)*, the *Muscle Spindle Cell Reflex (MSC)*, and the *Crossed Extensor Reflex*.

RELAXATION – The state of emotionless readiness where the mind is calm yet sharp, breath controlled yet directed with spirit steady yet motivated.

REVERSE MOTION – "Returning on the same path of an initiated move." Applying intention to a motion's opposite direction. The reverse motion of a straight punch is a back elbow, etc. Differentiate from *Opposite*.

RHYTHM – A regular repeated pattern of movement or sound. In partner dance for example this movement is cooperative where in fighting it is uncooperative with possible interruptions or cadence changes. See *Broken Rhythm* to differentiate.

RIDING THE STORM – The state of surviving a bad position, usually until the attempt is given up on or an escape route is created or observed.

ROOTED – Mental image of the feet connected firmly with the ground in place or moving. Some styles visualize roots growing from the bottoms of their feet into the ground. See *Balance* Pg 65.

ROTATION – Applied whole-body torque done by twisting of the body in one direction, then perhaps untwisting it in the other direction to increase force of action. See *Physical Principles* chapter, Pg 131.

SANDWICHING – "This involves striking a target from opposite sides," "simultaneously," "both weapons supporting each other."

SCISSORING – "The use of both legs vice-like to squeeze an opponent's body...etc." The upper body *Force Couple* motion also uses this around a body part by trapping on two opposing sides between accelerated motions (Glancing Palm). See *Type 1 Lever* Pg 143.

SELF-CORRECTING – "The ability to consistently make sound and logical judgments and to act on them when analyzing movements" "from a thorough knowledge of [martial art] principles, concepts & theories."

SEQUENTIAL FLOW – "This involves utilizing every conceivable natural weapon logically available within the movements of a technique sequence." See also *Compounded Energy, Kinetic Chain,* and *Wave Transference.*

SET – A choreographed pattern designed to practice a category of Basics. Stance Sets practice stances, Kicking sets practice kicks, Blocking sets practice blocking, etc. See *Form* to differentiate and the *Sets & Forms* chapter in the *Body.*

SETUP – A preliminary movement to create an opening or opportunity.

SETTLING – "The gradual sinking of your body weight and height each time you alter the width or depth of your stance. It is a method of solidifying your base." See *Momentum, Inertia,* and *Body Alignment.*

SET POINT – A timing method popularized and taught by the late Karate legend Joe Lewis, and used by many stand up fighters, that recognizes the moment weight is shifting from one foot to the other as a power void where vulnerability exists. See *Sport Fighting* chapter in the *Body.*

SHADOWBOXING – A term popular in Boxing and Kickboxing that refers to sparring with an invisible opponent. It can be done with a freestyle mindset or have a specific theme. This is the *Form* training of most sport fighting styles. See *Sport Fighting* chapter in the *Body.*

SHORTENING THE CIRCLE – "A method of moving up the circle to gain more reach." Cutting the angle of a circular path on the ground using footwork (Detouring the Kick) or in-the-air by changing the size and perhaps shape of a circle to increase its speed and range to impact (Snapping Arm).

SIMULTANEOUS – "Occurring, doing, or existing at the same time."

SPHERICAL MOTION – Circular motion encompassing every degree of space within the three physical dimensions, or 360° squared.

SPEED – Ed Parker's Concept with 3 Types: See Pg 75.
* Perceptual Speed – The minds time to perceive a situation.
* Mental Speed – The minds time to determine the course of action.
* Physical Speed – The time it takes for the body to react.

SPOTTING – The act of focusing the eyes on a point either in space or on an object/person to regain perspective for balance and for the accuracy of impacting a target. This is usually taught after turning or spinning around (and a common dance term) but is useful with or without that.

STAGES OF LEARNING – 4 Stages: Ed Parker's "3 Stages of Learning" +1:

<u>PRIMITIVE / EMBRYONIC</u> – "Early stage of development where moves are crudely executed."

MECHANICAL – "Where movements are clarified and defined, and thus, given meaning and purpose. Movements at this stage, however, are applied mechanically, and a student is more equipped to verbalize answers than to utilize them physically."

SPONTANEOUS – "Where the student's reactions are executed naturally, impulsively and without restraint, effort, or premeditation." This is where muscle memory leads mental memory.

EXTEMPORANEOUS – This overlaps the *Spontaneous Stage* and is where the mind is ahead of movement to adjust with situational analysis, body language recognition, pre-emptive action, and timing.

STANCES – The many ways of standing as part of overall posture and how the grounds leverage is transferred through the legs. See *Basics* Chapter in the *Body*.

STOP-HIT – A term borrowed from fencing that also applies in empty-handed fighting where the opponent is countered with a strike simultaneously as their attack is avoided (Fatal Variation).

STRANGLE – The technical term to describe an external attack that squeezes or constricts the neck, especially used to cause death. See *Choke/Chokehold* to differentiate.

STRATEGY – A plan of action used to achieve one's objective. See *Objective* and *Tactic* to differentiate, Pg 58.

STRESS RESPONSE – How we react when under stress from the obvious increase in heart rate and breathing to the less obvious liver glucose release and hypothalamus signals releasing hormones to our pituitary gland (ACTH) and adrenal medulla (cortisol). Other terms associated are *Fight or Flight, Tunnel Vision, Auditory Exclusion, Sympathetic Nervous System Response, Adrenal Stress Response, Body Alarm Reaction (B.A.R.)*.

People handle various levels of stress differently based upon personality, adrenal fitness, life experience, and/or any de-sensitivity training.

STRETCH REFLEX ACCELERATION – Aka, *Muscle-Tendon Elasticity*. This is the natural return action of a stretched muscle whose Potential Energy can be used to make for rapid muscular acceleration. This utilizes the natural stretch reflex inside a joint and muscle tissue after being extended, bent, or twisted.

STRIKES – Any move that hits but in Kenpo terminology this describes hitting with the hands and arms that are not punches or kicks, which have their own categories. See *Basics* chapter in the *Body*.

STRIKING POWER – The application of *Velocity, Leverage,* and *Torque* coordinated and synchronized with breath, intention, and mental focus.

STRONG LINE – Foot and body alignment that provides the greatest resistance against oncoming force or pressure, generally with one foot behind the other perpendicular toward the pressure with variances relative to exact positioning. See *Balance* and *Weak Line* to differentiate.

STRUCTURAL ALIGNMENT – Using the aligned musculoskeletal structure as a brace to create or maintain space; a striking or pushing surface used to attack a target; or a blocking surface to resist incoming force.

STRUCTURAL REINFORCEMENT – Connecting one of our anatomical structures to another of ours or an opponent's structure or a nearby surface. This can enable a more powerful attack, solidify a grip, provide greater resistance against incoming force, or be used as a launching platform.

STYLE – "The manner in which an individual applies and executes the System he has learned. Although underlying principles are the same, they are nevertheless altered to suit the individual." See *System* to differentiate.

SWEEP – Moving an opponent's foot from its stationary position on the ground, usually with your foot or leg. See *Buckle* and *Trip* to differentiate and the *Basics* chapter in the *Body*.

SYMMETRY – The exact correspondence of form on opposite sides of a dividing line, a plane, or about a center axis giving visual harmony as a result of even arrangement and balance.

SYNCHRONIZED – Occurring at the same time or simultaneously.

SYNONYM – A language term describing something with a similar meaning to something else. Basics with multiple applications, like an inward blocking motion used as a hammerfist or vertical elbow strike making them all synonymous with this motion. Ed Parkers quote that "many answers lie in a single move" surmises this concept succinctly. See *Analogy* and *Metaphor* to differentiate.

SYSTEM – "The unification of related concepts, truths, and basic elements of a particular school of Martial Arts." See *Style* to differentiate and the *System, Style, or Art* chapter in the *Spirit* book.

TACTIC – A maneuver used to help accomplish a strategy. See *Objective* and *Strategy* to differentiate, Pg 59.

TAILORING – "It entails two major aspects, (1) adjusting your physical as well as mental and emotional attitudes to fit each given situation; and (2) fitting moves to your body size, makeup, speed, and strength in order to maximize your physical efforts."

TANGENT – "The meeting of a straight line with a curved target" at a 90° angle to the center of the curve that then changes direction. A hook punch glancing through the jaw allowing for an inward elbow follow-up does this (Circling the Kick A).

TAP-OUT – A sport and training term where within a successfully applied hold or position the person being held 'pats' the other person, the ground, or themselves as a signal to stop. Note: A defeated street opponent may also have this option acknowledged to end the fight (i.e. saying "uncle" as from another time).

TECHNIQUE – In martial arts, doing an individual or combination of basics formulated into a pattern designed to accomplish a purpose. These can be applied on one or more than one-person, inanimate objects as in breaking, or in-the-air as when doing *Forms, Sets,* and *Shadowboxing.*

TEMPO – A rhythmic pattern of movement involving speed, regulated and adjusted in fighting to confuse and set up an opponent. It is used to keep an opponent guessing and to read or gauge their movement and openings.

TENDERIZING TECHNIQUES – The group of techniques to make an attacker want to relinquish a controlling hold, i.e. "soften him up." These include pinches, stomps, upward hook kicks or knees to the groin, head butts, biting, etc. The attack must be successfully defended. i.e. "riding the storm," in order to have the time to use these techniques.

THEN – A term that refers to the move that follows another move in a technique sequence. See *And* & *With* to differentiate.

THEORY – A system of assumptions based upon accepted principles as they relate to recognized Concepts or ideas. These are devised to analyze and explain the nature, purpose, and result of the subject being theorized about. See *Application* to differentiate.

TIMING – "The sophistication and punctuation of rhythm." For the martial artists this is viewed from the two main perspectives of *Movement Timing* and *Application Timing.* See *Mental Concepts* chapter, Pg 84.

Movement Timing is synchronizing related basics together to achieve maximum results. For any technique to reach its potential the application of mind (knowledge) with body (aligned technique with breath) and spirit (intention and focus) in unity is at the essence of this.

Application Timing is the live interaction between combatants regulated to create or hide openings, control the gap, or read another person's movement and reactions.

TORQUE – "Twisting and rotating action used to position your body and muscles to work at maximum efficiency." See Physical Principles chapter, Pg 131.

TOUCH REFLEX – The hardwired retraction of limbs, or other body parts, from excessive stimulation. Withdrawing the hand after touching a hot stove is the classic example. See *Crossed Extensor Reflex* to differentiate.

TRACKING – Two primary definitions:
1) A method of *Contouring* that normally follows ours or an opponent's limb into a target, or line of action. See *Guidelining* to differentiate.

2) The precise path a properly executed strike travels towards and into a target, then the retraction or return path to the original or next *Point of Origin*.

TRACTION – The connecting friction between objects that allows for leveraged force and acceleration to push or pull. It often involves the bottoms of the feet with the ground, but other body parts also interact in this way during standup and ground grappling.

TRAINING – Working out in the context of one's athletic activity to increase cardiovascular endurance, build muscular strength and muscle memory, improve functional flexibility, and gain experience.

A martial artist could do style specific exercises, pre-arranged patterns, freestyle shadowboxing, and sparring; along with running, weightlifting, and have an adjusted diet. See *Practice* to differentiate.

TRANSITION – Moves between moves, i.e. getting from one position to another. Continuously and efficiently connecting one effort to another, especially if checked or countered, is the highest level of any movement skill. Footwork involves weight transfer; striking involves connecting, redirecting, or utilizing a pre-loaded alternative weapon; grappling involves moving to the next most advantageous position. Timing enhances all.

TRAP – A checking method for attack or defense that catches then either holds or clears a natural weapon to minimize its use and create openings. Example: Grabbing and moving an opponent's high lead hand with our lead hand to create a head opening for a follow-up rear hand punch. See *Basics* and *Sport Fighting* chapters in the *Body*.

TRIANGLE – 3 combined angles adding up to 180º differentiated by the number of equal sides. 3 types: *Equilateral* (3 equal sides), *Isosceles* (2 equal sides) and *Scalene* (no equal sides). They are also known by angles contained as *Right* (one 90º angle), *Obtuse* (one angle bigger than 90º) and *Acute* (all angles less than 90º).

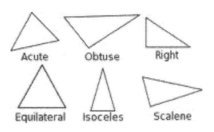

TRIP – Moves that affect balance by entangling the feet and legs. Pushing, pulling, or guiding an opponent over a strategically placed or applied leg or by picking up a foot or leg. See *Sweep* and *Buckle* to differentiate.

UNINTENTIONAL MOVES – "Unanticipated reactionary moves on the part of an opponent that, although accidental or unplanned, can cause injury if they remain unchecked." See *Intentional Moves* to differentiate.

UNIVERSAL PATTERN – Ed Parkers three-dimensional pattern showing the lines, circles, shapes, and paths of motion. See Mr. Parker's Infinite Insights Book 1 plus the *Physical Principles* chapter, Pg 122.

UNUSEFUL – Something that works occasionally in some circumstances but is not irreplaceable. Differentiate from *Useless* & *Useful*.

UPPER CASE MOVEMENT – Using upper body weapons or sections of the body to attack or defend. See *Lower Case* to differentiate.

USELESS – Something that does not work under any circumstances.

USEFUL – Something that works under many circumstances.

VARIABLE EXPANSION – "The ability to randomly select solutions, or build upon precepts, as a result of having a thorough knowledge of the principles and concepts of the Martial Arts."

VECTOR – The length and directional alignment of a linear path of movement determined by the speed/velocity, force, and distance it travels.

VELOCITY – "Time, rate, or speed of linear motion in a given distance." This also refers to the rapidity measure with which something covers the shortest distance between its initial and final positions and refers to the direction of change as well.

VIEWPOINT – "Viewing a confrontation from 3 points of view", yours, the opponent's, and a bystander's (witness). Many things and situations in life seen from these "viewpoints" allow for greater situational insight.

VISUALIZATION – Seeing in our minds eye a mental visual image or picture. This is done with varying degrees of definition based upon the clarity of recalling something already known or imagining something new. This is a powerful method used in martial arts, and other movement disciplines, to create mental images that give the mind familiarity and confidence.

WAVE TRANSFERENCE – The fluid progression of mechanical body movement as it accumulates through a path of a motion. This energy is compounded as it transfers in the body like a wave, generally from larger body areas to smaller ones. Using this process, the accumulation and compounding of body force builds into power at a point of impact. See also *Compounded Energy, Kinetic Chain,* and *Physical Principles* chapter, Pg 130.

WEAK LINE – The foot and body alignment on either side of an oncoming force or pressure that gives the least amount of support and resistance leaving an angle of imbalance. Differentiate from *Strong Line*.

WEB OF KNOWLEDGE – Created by Ed Parker, it prioritizes Kenpo Self-Defense Techniques by "the degree of difficulty in handling an attack." Ed Parker's 9 categories: *Grabs & Tackles, Pushes, Punches, Kicks, Holds & Hugs, Chokes & Locks, Weapons, Multiple Attackers, Combination Attacks.*

I prioritize these by range first, then by "degree of difficulty," or what I call "Severity of Attack." The order I use therefore is: *Grabs/Pulls, Pushes/Shoves, Punches/Strikes, Un-Natural Weapons, Kicks/Knees, Tackles/Takedowns, Holds (Hugs, Locks & Chokes),* and *Multiple Attackers*.

Knives, Clubs, and Guns (i.e. *un-natural weapons*) are after *Punches* since the range and attack path options are similar. *Tackles* are down the list as they are more dangerous than *Grabs* due to acceleration and potential body mass collision. *Holds* follow as natural follow-ups to a *Tackle* attempt. See *Self-Defense Technique* chapter in the *Body*.

WEDGE – Two lever arms forming a "V" shape that is used to open a narrow space or provide a bracing angle. See *Pry* to differentiate and *Physical Principles* chapter, Pg 145.

WELD – Connecting an opponent's body part to our self, creating a lever. Attaching (welding) their wrist to our hip before applying elbow pressure does this. See *Back Stop* to differentiate.

WHITE DOT FOCUS – A white dot on a black background symbolizing total focus. See *Black Dot Focus* to differentiate and *Mental Concepts* chapter, Pg 73.

WITH – Simultaneous coordinated movements. This is a slight variation from Mr. Parker's definition of, "it involves dual movements," by allowing more uses of the term. See *And* & *Then* to differentiate.

WORK – The amount of *Energy* transmitted to move a given target. See *Force* and *Power* to differentiate.

ZONES OF PROTECTION – See *Physical Principles* chapter, Pg 87.

ZONES OF SANCTUARY – "Dead areas of space where you can position yourself for protection." The classic Kenpo example recognizes the corners outside a circular club swing where the weapon does not reach (Returning Club). There are also inside zones that fit in this category. See *Physical Principles* chapter, Pg 95.

MENTAL CONCEPTS
Chapter III

Mental Concepts are how the mind thinks, focuses, directs, and understands. This is crucial in developing ourselves from the inside out, especially in martial arts. Without a proper mental framework and awareness to understand principles of physical movement then good technique and physical power would never be fully realized, like clapping the air with one hand, no sound.

This "Internal" (Yin) training is where mental concepts, understandings, and practices help optimize the *Physical Principles* of movement and applied technique covered in the next chapter. Individually and collectively, they can greatly contribute to the growth and prowess of a martial arts practitioner.

Some of these concepts are easily understood and can provide instant benefits, with some developing more slowly and continuously over time, and some require guidance and instruction to fully grasp.

19 *Mental Concepts* are listed and discussed in this chapter.

The first group consists of thoughts and visuals that occur, are felt, and developed through our minds understanding, interpretation, appreciation, and comprehension. These are *Motivation, Intention, Yin-Yang, Qi/Chi, Breath,* and *Planning (OST) - Objectives/Strategies/Tactics.*

The second group consists of an awareness within our minds awareness that relates to the application of our physical movement, and that can also be used relative to other structures and variables. These are *Posture, Balance, Focus, Speed, Power,* and *Directions & Angles.*

The third group consists of mental factors that only occur relative to another person or structure. These are *Distance & Timing, Dimensions & Zones, Contouring, Targets, Weapons, Equation Formula,* and *Levels of Force.*

MOTIVATION

This is the driving force to all we pursue and achieve in life. It can come at us from the outside such as an instructor, trainer, or drill sergeant barking commands or from inside as an inspiration bubbling up deep inside our psyche. Additionally, thoughts can motivate us, and external situations can inspire us with these all contributing to our effort, desire, or incentive to take some action.

Wherever this drive comes from, it is a motivational force that gives us the determination to accomplish short or long-term goals by seeing then having the energy to pursue an objective through to completion.

A coach or karate teacher can motivate us to do more push-ups or punches with forceful commands but if we share in the goal or vision that these develop of being stronger or a better puncher then we would work harder to do more pushups or punches, even when nobody is watching.

Positive and negative things, events, and people can inspire this passion that motivates us to work hard towards a goal. As humans we need these to tap into emotional reserves to help finish or exceed what others, or perhaps even we, had believed could be accomplished.

Without motivation it is easy to quit when things become difficult and challenging. Lifetime accomplishments like finishing school or getting a Black Belt would be impossible and daunting with unexpected life events like having to fight another person overwhelming.

Even though we "like" successes to occur this "liking" should not be confused with "wanting." "Liking" means we would take it if it came whereas "wanting" makes us put in the work to get it. This relates to any goal or lifelong pursuit, and it also relates to fighting where a motivated person may not quit until there is no life left in him or her.

Some refer to this quality as "competitive spirit" or "having heart" but these terms all describe the same refusal-to-quit quality. As my friend and former fight coach Orned "Chicken" Gabriel always said, "Winners never quit, and quitters never win" (Vince Lombardi actually said it, but I heard it first from Chicken).

This can also be termed a "will-to-win" or "will-to-succeed." It can come from a desire to prove something to others or oneself. However derived, this quality must be present to accomplish a challenging task. Fighting a worthy adversary is a challenging task that requires a large amount of competitive drive and determination to finish.

A strong-willed, determined, powerful, durable, aggressive, athletic, mean, scary opponent with a desire to cause harm can test anyone's heart and desire to survive. With a powerful desire and the competitive drive to succeed, win, or survive this challenge then technique and training can be the difference to overcoming such an adversary. Without this driving force of will the mere practice and knowledge of some martial arts can give a false sense of security.

With that determination in place a key goal in martial arts is to train so we don't have to think. This gets the mind and emotions out of the way so the body can react without the mind sabotaging the body and spirit by overthinking or by getting "psyched out." This is an area where sport fighting can be useful as it provides opportunities to practice and develop this valuable quality while learning about our self.

"Good" fight coaches know this so whether a developed or innate quality (probably a combination of both) a person's confidence and determination can be initially fragile when under duress. This psychological strength must be nurtured and built with challenged success opportunities over time until a fighter/person becomes mentally unbeatable thus making his or her physical skill even more formidable.

Tests that press the threshold of our known limits are a key to building what in martial arts is referred to as an "indomitable spirit," or one that is "incapable of being overcome, subdued, or vanquished; unconquerable."

This level of motivation and determination, whether inspired by events in one's life, driven and forged by a coach/instructor from the outside, or a combination of both is the internal strength needed and used to overcome life's difficult tests and challenges without quitting.

The will to win and the determination to never quit makes any fighter/person a serious and formidable adversary. It is a quality we want not only for use in martial artists but in life.

INTENTION

One of the most powerful forces in the universe is the *Intention* behind an action. It is what an effort is focused on accomplishing, its aim, purpose, or goal. Anything done without this intention is by definition "unintentional." Although sometimes it's better to be lucky than good this is not a basis for improvement or consistency.

Intention closely utilizes focus and influences everything in life from the biggest goals to "in the moment" behaviors. When applied as a *Mental Intention*, or mindful purpose, it can be the catalyst for a *Physical Intention* as used in martial arts.

Mental Intention
The application of any martial arts technique has more potential for success if the mind directs its use. Biological creatures have a level of consciousness that is reflexively reactive but in humans this can be developed and enhanced through instruction and repetitive training. This then becomes the "mind of no mind," or "mushin" sought in martial arts, but gained through insight and correct practice, all of which takes *Mental Intention*.

Without this intention whatever happens occurs unintentionally or accidentally and without expectation from that physical effort, or the ability to regulate it. Harm may or may not be the intent but without mental intention we are not in control.

The mind therefore should be motivated, decisive, and focused while engaging our *Qi* and spirit to direct our body into an action designed to accomplish a desired result. This becomes our *Physical Intention* directed by our *Mental Intention*. An eloquent Chi Gung principle describing this phenomenon by an author unknown to me is:

"The mind is the presence of intention, the eyes are the focus of intention, movement is the action of intention, breath is the flow of intention."

The intention or reason to learn, practice, and especially to use martial arts defines the discipline, techniques, strategies, and tactics preferred by an individual. These fall under the four primary categories of Military, Law Enforcement, Self-Defense, and Sport, as previously covered.

Military arts train to aggressively incapacitate or kill an enemy. Law Enforcement arts attack with the intention to contain, subdue, and probably arrest a criminal. Self-Defense arts practice with an intention of not fighting in normal day-to-day life or even contending with another person, and with an awareness of moral and legal repercussions. Sport arts train to fight in specialized aspects with legal/illegal techniques specified and rules for safety which all help determine a winner.

All these training intentions have overlapping techniques but differ in purpose with each also practicing techniques not used by the others. Difficulties can occur when someone trained in one martial intention finds themselves in a situation requiring a different one. This requires regulation so as not to do too much or too little.

The spectrum from where a controlling or non-injury method would suffice to a life or death situation is wide. Legal concerns may require less force or if appropriate the old philosophy "It's better to be tried by 12 then carried by 6," may suffice. Regardless, a choice of intention needs to be made.

Someone trained in a military style dealing with a drunken relative at a family party would need to make an intention adjustment. A sport fighter in a life and death street fight against multiple attackers, perhaps with weapons, would need a more lethal intention.

A "round" mentality as needed in sport fighting must be eliminated. Opponents need to be dropped quickly and not get up as nobody is obliged to help if you are injured, tired, or wanting to stop. This survival mentality includes vicious dirty fighting techniques against vital targets as the intention becomes to not "fight fair."

The heat of battle is not the time to determine whether or not you believe in capital punishment. It is therefore important to program our minds and train our body to avoid confusion and hesitation at a critical moment as any hesitation can allow for serious harm to occur to others or our self.

This means our personal value systems should be known in advance. Hopefully, a higher skill level and experience can give us more options and control over our self and our environment, but we are all human and vulnerable.

I tell women's self-defense class attendees that "your life and that of your family members are more valuable than that of a criminal intent on beating, raping, or killing you. They do not deserve your compassion. Poke the eyes to blind, strike the groin to rupture, kick the knees to cripple." The choice is ultimately theirs, but they should understand and evaluate them up front.

I then have them visualize their worst nightmare attacking them and ask, "are you willing to, and without remorse, grab one of his eye balls, rip it out of his head, throw it on the ground and stomp it like a grape?" This always results in squeamish looks but becomes a reality check that helps them focuses on the mental frame needed to survive a ferocious brutal attack.

If they have trouble visualizing being that vicious, I have them think of their children, parents, siblings, pets, or who/whatever they love more than themselves as being attacked. Any apprehension seems to vanish as everyone can then summon a higher level of intensity. We can then move forward with the business of learning technique.

The "7 Levels of Force" at the end of this chapter covers the span of these choices for applying physical technique that once decided can aid in learning to apply an appropriate technique to deal with a specific situation.

Learning, practicing, and training to use these different intentions requires discipline and control so partners are not seriously injured. Those practicing martial arts together should always know and agree on the intention of their training so positive progress can be made and nobody gets hurt.

A training session occurs with a mutually agreed upon level of contact with mutually agreed upon ranges of fighting, and with agreed upon weapons to mutually accepted targets. Hopefully a third person is available to supervise and regulate the action.

This is training so it can be hard yet still must be safe and perhaps fun, but never personal. Without ground rules and compatible training partners bad things can happen. The intention in training is to NOT HURT TRAINING PARTNERS! Here are four reasons why you must train with a safe intention in these environments:

1) It's not nice to hurt family members, friends, classmates, or anyone else who trusts you to have good control while practicing.
2) If you injure a training partner(s) temporarily or permanently you can't get better because you need them to improve.
3) When an injured training partner recovers they probably won't want to train with you and again, you need training partners to improve.
4) If you are unable to hurt a tough training partner you have another set of problems because you may be in danger of getting hurt by them.

The bottom line is that training can be intense and hard, but training partners should not be intentionally hurt, and practice should be done only with people who understand this concept.

Through understanding and practice the application of mental intention allows us to train in the discipline(s) that help us accomplish our goals, while staying healthy. The ability to use an appropriate level force in a real-life environment is only improved through this focused mental intention.

Physical Intention
Once the mind has its intention or purpose the body must physically execute the action. This *Physical Intention* is the timing, accuracy, structural alignment, and force needed to accomplish the objective. These are the learned and rehearsed techniques of martial arts.

Intention is a broad subject where the interaction of two intentions can be cooperative, or one intention can be unintentionally blocked by another, or perhaps the intention is to block another person's intention. This is the human dynamic on display in all things where people interact. Ultimately, we can only control our self so doing things with intention is the best way to accomplish any task efficiently and effectively.

In Physics, Sir Isaac Newton described "laws of motion" with the first being "a body continues in its state of rest, or of uniform motion in a right line, unless it is compelled to change that state by forces impressed upon it." While this is true of inanimate objects moving through space it is not always true for people and animals that are moving themselves voluntarily through space, and perhaps with intention.

Fakes, feints, and angular adjustments are just a few of the many options a person uses to challenge Newton's first law. The same motion or movement can have different intentions such as to break or tear tissue, dislocate a joint, make someone unconscious, hold to control, win a competition with rules and sportsmanship, or be non-martial art related.

In martial arts however, a correctly applied physical intention is crucial to applying the mental intention sought to accomplish an objective. This *Physical Intention* is what the study of martial arts technique is about and covered in some detail throughout this book series.

YIN/YANG

This philosophy dates back in the ancient Chinese culture to at least the 7th Century BCE with the *I Ching* or *Book of Changes* with its broken and unbroken lines. The iconic black and white yin/yang symbol or Tai Ji, i.e. grand ultimate, synonymous with Taoism came later.

The roots of this Taoist philosophy come from the *Tao Te Ching* written by Lao Zi around the 6th Century BC where one of his many quotes is "the one (the Way/Tao) begot the two (Yin-Yang) that begot the three (Rule of Threes) that begot the ten-thousand things (Everything)."

It is a key diagnostic tool used in Traditional Chinese Medicine (TCM) and the philosophical foundation for Chinese martial arts at the root of much of the world's known systems and styles.

This simple, yet all-encompassing concept relates all things and purposes into complimentary opposites. They define each other in relative terms and are only useful in relationship to each other.

"*Difficult* and *Easy* complement each other"
"*Long* and *Short* define each other"
"*High* and *Low* oppose each other"
"*Front* and *Back* follow each other" etc.

Yin-Yang Comparisons / Relative Complimentary Opposites

YIN	YANG
Earth - Low - Down	Heaven - High - Up
Substance - Blood	Energy - Qi
Night - Dark - Cold	Day - Light - Hot
Passive - Female - Soft - Absorbing	Active - Male - Hard - Penetrating
Minus - Negative	Plus - Positive
Closed - Concealed - Contract	Open - Overt - Expand
Inhalation - Internal	Exhalation - External
Innate Instinct	Acquired Skill
Circles / Circular	Lines / Linear
Zero - Even	One - Odd
Left - Front - Lower - Medial Body	Right - Back - Upper - Lateral Body

This broad and deep subject is only briefly touched upon here with a few martial art references. All movement and applications can however be explained and analyzed using yin/yang and its 4 types of interaction.

Awareness of this concept allows the mind to discover, understand, and relate different yin-yang aspects. This foundation can simplify and help categorize elements of training, teaching, or be used towards any purpose.

4 Types of Yin-Yang Interaction

Opposition

This describes two opposite components at either end of a cycle, like seasons of the year. It can also mean things on a relative continuum of energy or matter, so water is a Yin substance relative to steam, but is Yang relative to ice.

In anatomy and physiology study each muscle has a complimentary opposing muscle, so the bicep muscle used to pull (yin) is balanced by the tricep muscle used to push (yang). These motions are also balanced so the bicep muscle does a concentric contraction to bend where the tricep does a concentric contraction to straighten.

In movement this opposition can be seen in that as the right shoulder moves forward the left shoulder moves back, making for simultaneous forward and reverse motions.

Interdependence

Nothing is totally yin or yang as each contains the beginning of the other, and they cannot survive without each other. Notice the symbol contains some yin within yang (black dot inside white area) and yang within yin (white dot inside black area).

Day and night are constantly evolving and coexisting, there is no energy without matter, no out-breath without in-breath and vice versa, etc.

In martial arts this can mean being soft and pliable when defending yet not yielding, or firm and hard when attacking yet able to adjust and adapt upon meeting resistance.

Mutually Consuming and Supportive

The relative levels of yin and yang are continuously changing so they are never static. This can be a balanced natural change like daytime gradually consuming the night, or night consuming the day.

They can also be out of balance where a strong muscle overused or damaged suddenly becomes weak, or a weak relaxed muscle suddenly explodes with energy.

In TCM this becomes one of the four pillars of diagnosis used to help evaluate a patient's imbalance. That pillar assesses a patient having too much or a preponderance of something is seen as *excess yin* or *excess yang* where not having enough or a weakness of something is seen as *deficient yin* or *deficient yang*. The goal in the healing arts is to help return the system to a state of balance and harmony, or homeostasis.

In movement disciplines like martial arts this can refer to how a tight and hard muscle structure (yang) inhibits or consumes smooth movement (yin) and how soft movement without an intended direction from the muscle structure can be ineffective and even become damaged.

Contrarily a relaxed structure (yin) explodes more easily (yang) and is directed more smoothly (yin) into an explosive impact (yang).

Inter-Transformation
How yin changes into yang and vice versa evolving in its own time and not randomly. An embryo (yin) needs heat and warmth (yang) to grow into a child but applying heat and warmth to any random substance will not produce that same result.

This can be seen in physical, mental, and emotional development, whether it is a child crawling before walking or a martial arts practitioner learning basic skills before progressing into advanced skills. This process requires patience that must be accepted, guided, and evolved at every level.

QI/CHI/KI (Chee)

Covered briefly here is the extensive topic of Qi. This multifaceted concept can be difficult, illusive, or even controversial for some to grasp. The existence of Qi is fundamental to Chinese medicine and, whether an individual accepts the concept or not, it is part of how a martial artist develops internal health and external power.

Some say they "don't believe" in Qi, but since Qi is a concept it is not important to believe in it to have it, or perhaps it is thought of differently or called by a different name. This discussion presumes the existence of Qi.

The Western mind often understands Qi as internal energy or heat inside the body, and this can work as a basic concept. For the scientific mind Qi can be thought of as the protons, neutrons, and electrons relationship to each other in a cell or the role of the mitochondria in energizing cells, but it goes much deeper as this product called Qi is greatly influenced by the intention of the person it is contained within.

Qi can be cultivated and developed with the minds direction by guiding the breath and, in martial arts, is also combined with external physical movement. This practice over time incrementally builds the Qi, relative to the person, into an internal force that can be directed by the mind inside the body to prevent Qi stagnation and for healing or to provide resistance to attack, or outwardly through movement as projected energy.

TCM (Traditional Chinese Medicine) theory says, "Qi is the commander of blood and blood is the mother of Qi" (meditate on that one). TCM also has a useful big picture concept of Qi that illustrates human health called "Pre-Natal Qi" and "Post-Natal Qi."

Pre-Natal Qi is the constitution and genetics passed on to us by our biological parents at conception then nurtured through the birth process. *Post-Natal Qi* is what we or others put into and do with our bodies after birth and throughout life, including air, water (liquids), and food (solids). See *Nutrition* chapter in the *Spirit*. Additionally, lifestyle, behavior, unforeseen injury, and illness are factors in our *Post-Natal Qi*.

Pre-Natal Qi is loosely analogous to the voltage and current in a rechargeable battery, our personal battery in this case. Some people are born "D" batteries, and some are "AAA" with every size in between, and relative to each other so a "AAA" might be a "D" relative to someone else.

Post-Natal Qi is the nurturing, or lack of, that happens throughout our life. If born with a robust "D" battery constitution the potential exists to keep recharging to that level throughout life. Whatever the constitutional size and potential of our "battery," the goal would be to optimize our genetic potential through diet and lifestyle.

The "AAA" can't become the relative "D" but it can stay charged more consistently or longer than a weaker "D" constitution. Although potentially capable of more power, a "D" constitution could energetically and physically deteriorate to a weaker "AAA" from poor lifestyle and/or disease.

Continuing this analogy, the current (Qi) can be nurtured, developed, maintained, directed and, unlike a battery improved upon. Qi building exercises (like martial arts), proper diet, rest, good thoughts, and healthy breathing (see *Breath* section) all contribute to overall health.

Note: A popular TCM technique uses moxa (artemesia / mugwort) to heat points on the body, aka moxibustion, to build Qi. The primary point for longevity, improving the immune system, and Qi building is *Stomach 36 / Zu San Li / Leg 3 Mile,* perhaps meaning one can walk 3 more miles after this point is treated. Lower abdominal point CV6 / Qi Hai / Sea of Qi and others are also treated using this technique to help build Qi.

As Qi is maintained, and hopefully increased over time, it can then be guided inside our body using our mind to direct it with our breath for different purposes. For example, think about your right little finger now! Your mind just put Qi there. Now use any of the breathing techniques from the section on *Breath* to focus your Qi to your right little finger, or wherever you want as this can be done anywhere in the body and improved upon over time.

Relate this idea to learning how to punch. A martial artist understands how a new skill, like a punch, is not as good the first time as the hundredth (presuming good technique of course), which is not as good as the thousandth. "I fear not the man who has practiced 10,000 kicks once, but the man who has practiced one kick 10,000 times." – Bruce Lee, or a story attributed to him that "before starting in martial arts a punch was a punch and a kick was a kick, but with instruction a punch was no longer a punch and a kick no longer a kick, then after achieving a level of expertise a punch was once again a punch and a kick was once again a kick." More meditation is recommended to fully comprehend that explanation as it applies to learning any skill.

All physical motions, from swinging a baseball bat to playing a musical instrument to all martial art movements improve through correct repetition using this alignment of Qi with the musculoskeletal structure, nervous system, breath, mental focus, and intention, all nurtured by the blood.

Martial arts also use this alignment of Qi to generate explosive power in ways to affect someone else's Qi (see the *Body, Pressure Point* chapter). A training goal would then be to build our Qi, maintain a healthy constitution, direct our Qi internally for self-healing, or outwardly if needed.

BREATH

Breathing as we know is fundamental to human life. An *Inward* breath (inhaling Oxygen) is the first thing we do when born with an *Outward* breath (exhaling Carbon Dioxide) the last thing we do in life, and every moment in between spent breathing *In* or *Out* (Nitrogen is also involved in both breath directions). As I often tell students bowing into or out of a class, "breathe in, breathe out, air is good."

It's been said that we get only a certain number of breaths, and heartbeats, in life so breathe slowly and deep while keeping your heart from racing when possible. Breath in the martial arts context is often synonymous with Qi, described in the previous section. This Qi needs oxygen to enrich the blood that it then travels with.

Since everyone instinctively inhales and exhales the perception is that everyone breathes well but this is generally not the case. Breathing can be very sophisticated and is a very deep (pun intended) and studied subject, yet ignorance abounds.

Breathing is first understood in the mind then developed and directed for use in the body. Structurally and mechanically understanding how the organ of breathing, the lungs, receives and releases air is useful.

The lungs do not draw air inwards as this task is accomplished by the diaphragm muscle contracting. This umbrella shaped muscle is under the lungs and heart (upper jiao or clean mist area) but above the stomach, liver, spleen, etc. (middle jiao or muddy/bubbling pool area).

The diaphragm muscle contracts downward on the *in-breath* to help the lungs expand and draw air in. The lungs contract and compress on the *out-breath* with help from the abdominal muscles and a relaxing diaphragm muscle to release or push the air out of the lungs.

Athletes, singers, musicians, and others train to refine, control, channel, and project air through their body, voice, or instrument. Martial arts also have a long tradition of understanding and efficiently utilizing breath and breathing techniques. These are done not only for external focus, as used with fighting technique, but also for building robust internal health.

Breath practice ranges from soft flowing relaxation to hard dynamic tension and everything in between. Training the breath in this context is directed by the mind so not only does it build Qi but teaches how to move and direct this energy internally.

Note: Due to a long history of meditative practices emphasizing sophisticated breathing techniques this training is often associated with Eastern religious teachings. A religious affiliation however is not a prerequisite to practicing or having good breathing technique, although much can be learned from what has been developed in this regard.

Concept of Breath
The *in-breath* is generally done through the nose with the *out-breath* done through the nose or mouth depending on the purpose. Many ideas, theories, and opinions on effective and proper breathing techniques exist but they come down to the two main concepts of *Soft* and *Hard* breath.

Soft breathing also goes by *relaxed, natural, normal, Buddhist* and *yogic.* Hard breathing is also called *reverse, effort/exertion,* and *Taoist.* The terms *soft* and *hard* will be used here but however referred a martial artist should understand both as each will be used.

Soft breathing techniques resemble how a baby breathes and how we should breathe throughout our normal daily activities and when we sleep. This is when the relaxed abdomen expands (belly button moving away from spine) as the lungs fill up with air on the *in-breath* then collapses (belly button moving towards spine) and empties on the *out-breath.*

This *soft* breath can be done without meditation as in normal daily breathing. It can also be done with meditation while mindfully training and directing the breath through our body. Yoga practitioners often focus on the breaths entry point by vibrating the glottis in the throat. This is called Ujjayi breathing or "ocean sound."

Note: This breath can give the illusion the stomach is filling with air as the lungs and diaphragm muscle expand downward into the abdominal area. This application of breath is competing for space with the abdominal organs causing them to move out of the way. This internal organ movement is an added benefit of this breath as it gently massages the internal organs, keeping them vibrant with each breath.

The *hard* breath has the abdomen contract inward on the *in-breath* (belly button moving towards the spine) then expands to sink and push on the *out*-breath (belly button moves away from the spine). This is the natural direction of the breath when we exert force.

Test this by placing a hand below your navel then make any forceful exertion sound. You will feel a pressurized tightening and expansion of your lower stomach against your hand. Note: This should not be confused with the Valsalva maneuver of Western medicine.

This breath is used for lifting, striking, or absorbing contact as it contracts the muscles and body structures around the internal organs solidifying the torso for uniform action. A guttural sound like a grunt or growl accompanies this internal compression deep inside the body and is referred to as the "yell of the spirit" or "kiai" (key-eye) in martial arts.

The mind directs these breathing techniques, so combinations of *soft* and *hard* breaths exist with as many possibilities as concepts surrounding the direction of the inward and outward breath cycle. The volume of air *in* and *out* can also be regulated for different purposes.

Both techniques should be practiced in a relaxed way to avoid internal injury. And visually, as mentioned, in the *Soft* technique the belly button moves away from the spine on the *In-breath* then towards the spine on the *Out-breath* and on the *Hard* technique the belly button moves towards the spine on the *In-breath* then away from the spine on the *Out-breath*.

A useful TCM image is the *Triple Warmer / San Jiao / 3 (Triple) Burner* sections, and meridian channel. It contains upper (above diaphragm), middle (diaphragm to navel), and lower (navel to pelvic floor) sections with connecting points down the medial arms.

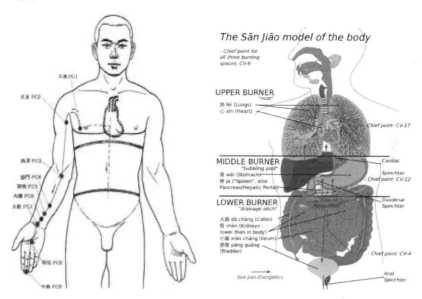

This concept has many uses in the practice of oriental healing where the upper jiao is visualized as a mist, the middle jiao like a bubbling or muddy pool, and the lower jiao as a drainage ditch. A martial artist could use it to reference target locations and angles of attack, but it can also provide a good image of how the breath is felt inside the body.

A breath cycle using the *soft* or *hard* method can take place in any one, two, or all three sections using this concept. A soft relaxed breath generally begins in the stomach (middle jiao) then moves up into the chest (upper jiao). Many people breathe primarily in their chests (upper jiao) which is a less healthy breath cycle.

A full and more productive breath cycle would be for the *In-breath* to feel like it starts in the lower then middle filling upwards to the upper section. The *out-breath* is reversed as the upper empties down into the middle and then lower sections.

This expansion and contraction of air inside our body physically moves and affects the lungs and nearby internal organs. The stomach, liver, spleen, pancreas, intestines, bladder, and kidneys can all benefit from a healthy breath cycle, with a bonus that every correct breath is like doing a relaxed sit-up as the abdominal muscle structure is utilized every time.

Whatever breathing method is practiced the development and growth of the accompanying internal Qi takes time. For this reason, it should be thought of as a lifelong endeavor. Patience and satisfaction with small progressions must be appreciated.

Proper technique is important so do not attempt to rush, tighten, or force results as that can be dangerous and even cause internal damage. Stop if pain or bad side effects, and always seek proper instruction.

Another useful TCM concept in this regard is expressed as "kidneys grasp the Qi." Remember that the diaphragm muscle draws air in and is located just above the kidneys so visualize them grasping and pulling the diaphragm down on the *in-breath*. The lungs, with help from the abdominal muscles, then contract on the *Out-breath* pushing air out as the kidneys relax.

Breathing techniques can be practiced lying, sitting, standing, walking, or be done with coordinated movement. Martial arts have emphasized a full array of these over the millennia but in all cases it is important the body posture is aligned to minimize obstruction to the breath (see *Posture*).

Energetically, meditative breathing techniques place the tongue tip at the roof of the mouth to connect the front of the body (yin or conception vessel line) with the back of the body (yang or governing vessel line). This is also the closest connection to stimulating the Pituitary Gland. The lips are lightly closed as the air moves in and out of the nose, although more vigorous movement often elicits a mouth exhale either projected outward or falling outward as in sighing.

Controlling breath and building air volume using the *soft* or *hard* method should be done slowly and reflectively. Depending on the purpose these can be done with or without body tension but is best done where an opportunity to listen inside without distraction, if possible. One technique covers the ears, possibly with the palms, while lying down to hear the breath move inside. This can be disconcerting to some but enjoyable silence for others.

The deepest *soft* or *hard* breath practice begins in the lower sections between the navel and pubic bone (dantien in TCM) or even lower in the perineum or pelvic floor. This *In-breath* fills the body upward (possibly to the upper chest) followed by the *Out-breath* emptying the body of air from the highest point down to the lower abdomen or perineum again.

This can be done either straight up and down within the body like an elevator where the air goes up then down, or better as a circular orbit moving up the back (yang side) on the *In-breath* circling over the head then down the front (yin side) on the *Out-breath*.

There are many visuals and analogies that martial artists, yoga experts, singing coaches, body builders, and others use that can be researched to learn and develop the breath using these *Soft* and *Hard* techniques. Breath practice gives various sensations from peaceful relaxation, to internal Qi movement, to dramatic physical explosiveness.

Here are a few mental concepts of *Soft* and *Hard* breathing that I have come across or thought of but are by no means the only ones. Some of these visuals can be used with either or both breathing methods.

The "One Side" at a time method is two-fold. First you could physically or through mental focus block one nostril then focus your breath cycle through the unblocked nostril, and/or breathe into one side of your body (any of the following breath cycle visuals can be used with this).

The "Accordion" visual is where the torso is imagined with this musical instrument inside. The ribs are felt to expand sideways on the *In-breath* then compress back together on the *Out-breath*.

The "Vertical Accordion" visual is where the torso is imagined with this musical instrument turned vertically inside. It expands open on the *In-breath* then compresses together on the *Out-breath*. This motion correlates with the movement of the diaphragm muscle and minimizes the shallow chest expansion breathing that is so common.

The "Balloon" visual is more for soft breathing where we see our body as a balloon. The nose is the opening as the lower abdomen expands on the *in-breath* as we feel the pressure increasing to the outer surface of our skin. When the air is released on the *out-breath* the balloon deflates relaxing the skin and compressing internally against the bones.

The "Reverse Balloon" works with the hard breath and where the bones are compressed on the *in-breath* as the navel moves towards the spine then released and expanded out towards the skin on the *out-breath*.

The "Water Pitcher" visual can be used with the soft or hard breath and where air is seen moving *In* like water filling up a pitcher. The water/air fills up the pitcher/us from the bottom to the top so as the air is siphoned *in* through our nose it fills our body from the stomach up to the chest. The *out-breath* sensation is as if a plug at the bottom of the pitcher were pulled so the water/air drains out emptying downward, yet as the air escapes through the nose or mouth.

The "Super Ball" visual works for either method. It sees a ball lifted upward on the *in-breath* then falling downward on the *out-breath* where it bounces off the pelvic floor then moving upward again repeating the cycle.

The "Belly Button" visual focuses on the direction of the navel while breathing. For the hard or reverse breath, it is pulled toward the spine on the *in-breath* then rebounds (bounces) off the spine forward on the *out-breath*. It would be the opposite for the soft breath.

The "Turkey Baster" is a hard breath visual with this utensil pictured upside down in the abdomen where the plunger is compressed on the *in-breath* then released/expanded on the *out-breath*.

The "Tea Kettle" analogy is a hard breath visual used by the late Kenpo Master Ed Parker. He relates the martial breath to steam building up and stored in a teakettle that is released through the spout as a steady flow of pressurized energy. If you take the lid off the kettle the steam dissipates, and the system must be re-pressurized.

The only problem with this visual is that a tea kettle is solid so maintains a constant shape and volume whereas the pliable human body expands and contracts. This allows for us to not only grow the potential volume through practice but to collapse around the air as we force it out, increasing the force of the pressure.

An eastern concept done with the *soft*, but possibly *hard* breath, is the *Small & Large Cosmic Orbit*.

The *Small Cosmic Orbit* visualizes Qi moving with the *in-breath* from the perineum (pelvic floor) up the tailbone to the dantien where on the *out-breath* it circles forward and down to the perineum again where the cycle restarts. This is akin to a turbine slowly spinning inside the lower abdomen generating heat (Qi).

The *Large Cosmic Orbit* does this same thing but on a whole-body scale. The Qi moves with the *in-breath* from the perineum up the GV/yang/back centerline meridian following the spine and over the head to where the tongue is connected at the pallet. The Qi moves with the *out-breath* from the root of the tongue down the CV/yin/front centerline meridian to the perineum where it restarts. These also correlate with the Hindu concept of Chakras.

These Cosmic Orbits are advanced mental breathing concepts that are a lifelong endeavor for some people and is said to take 20 plus years to develop where they can be felt and used internally, or perhaps even projected outwardly. This is part of how dynamic Qi energy is distributed to body parts as used for fighting and internal self-healing.

As with everything, not only knowledge but a talent and effort component are a determinant of success. Some people get this naturally and can achieve higher and higher levels while others may struggle, or never feel it. Everyone, however, can improve from where they start with knowledge and effort.

The key point is that through controlled and directed breathing air volume can be increased. This can bring many benefits including strengthening our Qi for martial arts power and internal health, calming our minds for lower stress and more rational thought. These all help us live a long and healthy life. With so many benefits, understanding breathing techniques and its practice should be part of every martial artist's mental and physical training.

Applying the Breath
Whatever the breathing method, when coordinated with movement as in martial arts there is a basic formula to follow. The *in-breath* is done when the intention of the arms move outward, upward, or backwards, and the *out-breath* when the intention of the arms move inward, downward, or forward.

Sophisticated martial arts systems use movement patterns with breath to help develop this timing and coordination of inside with outside which builds internal strength with external focus. Soft style martial arts like Yang Tai Chi generally move slowly and fluidly while using a soft breath technique, where a hard style like Shotokan Karate moves more rigidly while using the harder breath technique.

The slow-moving styles are normally done with the relaxed breath but breathing is flexible so the hard / reverse breath or even combined breath can be done. The breathing technique used would depend on the practitioner's intention while practicing although a full-speed powerful and focused martial art movement is most forcefully applied using the *hard* breath method.

Applying the breath in martial arts has other variables as well due to the variety of movements, timing, and force applied. These include the volume of breath exerted for a given move, with the exerted sounds used to optimize the use of those different volumes of air, and how many *Out-breaths* go with each *In-breath*.

In any case, the volume of breath used for an action is determined by the size of the movement. Small movements require a small exertion of air while large movements require a larger exertion of air. This air exertion is often accompanied by a sound that the body wants to do naturally if we let it. The exuded sound should match the breath and the activity. For example:

A small flicking move like a finger whip would get a short hiss of air from the tongue ("sss" sound).

A quick jabbing move would require a short burst of air from the mouth ("sh", "ai" or "hai" sound), or the nose as taught by many boxing coaches.

A driving power punch would demand a larger burst of air ("huh", "huss" or "oos" sound) like a growl.

A complete body movement such as a tackle would require a larger guttural effort ("uhh" sound), more like a roar.

The ratio of exerted *Out-breath* to gathered *In-breath* is analogous to singing a song in that one whole breath is not generally used to sing each note but rather is spread out over several notes before another *In-breath* is required. Practice by taking an *In-breath* then use the *Out-Breath* to sing several notes of varying lengths and tempos from the children's song "Row, Row, Row Your Boat."

<u>In-breath</u> - "row row row your boat gently down the stream"
<u>In-breath</u> - "merrily merrily merrily merrily life is but a dream"
To sing slower:
<u>In-breath</u> - "row row row your boat"
Short <u>In-Breath</u> - "gently down the stream"
<u>In breath</u> - "merrily merrily merrily merrily"
Short <u>In-breath</u> - "life is but a dream"

This is the same as with martial art movement in that one breath can feed several movements, some smaller and some larger. Of course, one whole breath can be utilized for one whole movement, but it would be a large movement like a tackle or a long drawn out hard movement, perhaps a fight ending strike.

The point is that the volume of air needed for the activity attempted may vary from one person to another and from one application to another, but the breath should match the movement(s) just as it matches the notes, tempo, and air capacity when singing a song.

Moving, as with singing, is better done when coordinated through a controlled active breath cycle regulated to and with the effort needed. This can become more difficult as the heart rate increases so a method to accommodate this increase is to bring rapid short bursts of air *In* through the nose then push rapid short bursts of air *Out* of the mouth.

This will vary depending on how "winded" we become. It can be done at a 2:1 ratio where 2 bursts of air are forced into the nose then 1 burst is forced out from the mouth. As we become more winded it could become 2:2 or 3:1 then progressively to 4:2, etc. as needed. This allows the air to be controlled by us, rather than *it* controls us.

Overall, it's beneficial to understand and develop the breath to control, direct, and regulate airflow inside our bodies for maximum performance and good health. Techniques like those discussed here can help us to understand and do that.

Experiment, research, and find what works for you. Remember that breathing can be developed, controlled, and directed to a high degree with knowledge and practice.

PLANNING – O.S.T.

Objectives – Strategies – Tactics

The subject of planning covers many things besides martial arts. Planning your career, finances, health and fitness, relational happiness, are but a few of many things that are done better with some intellectual foresight before moving forward. The formula for planning involves the three primary factors known as *Objectives*, *Strategies*, and *Tactics*.

Relating to martial arts or competing in anything, planning how to succeed can provide advantages over an adversary. This requires determining our ultimate goal (objective), then forming a plan of action (strategy), then implementing methods to achieve that plan (tactics).

Depending on what is being planned for as in a sport fighting competition compared to an on the spot self-defense situation can be the difference between several weeks or months of training and preparation to an on the spot assessment followed by action.

Whatever the time frame this plan can become the difference between victory and defeat, or in some circumstances life and death. Aside from the famous Mike Tyson quote that "everyone has a plan 'till they get punched in the mouth" does not take away the usefulness of starting with a plan.

This subject relates to what the late Kenpo Grandmaster Edmund K Parker called *Preparatory Considerations* in his writings addressing many aspects of this subject.

Objective – The Ultimate Goal

Different martial artists train with different goals in mind. Civilian practitioners should be learning, training, practicing, yet enjoying a peaceful life. Military and Law Enforcement personnel train with a sense of life or death urgency. Sport Fighters train to win a competition for trophies, medals, belts, money, fame, and/or for fun.

In all cases, if we must fight then our *objective* should be to try and win or perhaps just get away safely as in self-defense. Since sport fighting is done voluntarily with rules and guidelines it is covered extensively in my *Body* book chapter on that subject. The focus here therefore is more on the self-defense aspect.

If we get into a personal dispute, we should always be trying to help the other person to "save face" by not intentionally humiliating or embarrassing them. If involved in a criminal attack we cannot be naïve as to how a criminal might disguise setting us up or maybe they could be surprisingly blatant. In either case our objective must change from avoiding to winning and/or getting away safely.

A quote attributed to Mr. Parker summarizing his first *Preparatory Consideration* of *Acceptance* is "if you can't get out of a fight, then get into it." This is when conflict has not been avoided as we recognize physical force is our only feasible way out, making it a reality we must consciously accept.

A lack of acceptance is dangerous in a street confrontation since good people genuinely do not want to fight. It's easy for nice people to be in denial and wait too long to accept that this person (or people) is (are) giving us no choice but to physically fight them. This hesitation could leave us vulnerable, making this a critical moment where our objective and attitude must change if we want to get away safely.

Strategy – Plan of Action to Reach the Objective
In a tense situation where the *objective* is to avoid a physical fight a *strategy* could be to try and de-escalate the situation with words. This must be done while maintaining a safe distance with a hidden defensive posture, all while trying to help the adversary save face.

We are prepared to fight, and probably even strategizing how it could play out, yet still trying to avoid a physical altercation. Presuming the objective of avoiding did not work and we have accepted the reality that an adversary has now become an opponent so the strategy changes to what gives us the best chance of winning.

Generally, in sport fighting or even perhaps in war there is an opportunity to project and plan a strategy but in a spontaneous self-defense situation there is little or no time. Once accepted then who will make the first move becomes a consideration.

There is a possibility they will not make that first move but be satisfied with just getting in the last word. This is where our own ego can be tested by allowing someone to save face if possible, although difficult, it can help avoid physical conflict. A humiliated ego can make people (especially men) snap and do regretful things so nobody wins here.

Legally we probably should not attack first, but under some conditions this might be best *tactic*, perhaps against multiple opponents. The element of surprise does also have value, and with multiple opponents can help eliminate one guy right away while determining our next position in advance.

The legal repercussions should be taken into consideration if possible but can only occupy so much thought in this type of situation. Remember that old survival saying that, "It's better to be tried by 12 then carried by 6." The goal is survival first and the rest will sort out in time.

With proper space and checks in place then reasons to allow an opponent to move first could be legal but also to see how they move. This can give a trained person an idea of what they know, or do not know, about fighting along with alerting us to their strengths and weaknesses.

This "wait and see" method is the self-defense style school of thought that accepts an opponent is not attacking until they have committed to an action.

A trained, semi-pseudo-untrained attacker will prefer some method of attack. The untrained attack will be greatly exaggerated and telegraphed, with the semi and pseudo trained a little less obvious. The trained person could be at various levels of expertise in one or multiple disciplines, with their experience level probably unknown to us. These are the most dangerous people but luckily are not usually the ones to worry about, at least in a self-defense situation.

A semi-pseudo-untrained aggressor's first attack is often the overhand right or perhaps a tackle attempt. Observation and experience can help to recognize how someone's weight shift, posture, and range adjustment is done to set up these attacks. This awareness should be used to position our self so as not to get "sucker-punched" or taken down.

Even trained fighters favor the stance of their dominant style. This can help assess whether that is grappling or striking which can help us adjust range and perhaps know what they do not protect well. The *Preparatory Considerations* of *Range* and *Position* become important at this phase.

Some generalities are that boxers and kickboxers tend not to protect their groins well, grapplers are more susceptible to head strikes, with even cross trained fighters favoring an attack range or a progressive series of ranges.

In all cases someone solely trained as a sport fighter is not trained to defend eyes, ears, throat, groin, and small digit attacks, so these could become part of a strategy if fighting them, aside from any desire we may have to just test mano y mano capabilities against that person.

In any case, it takes awareness and adjustment to implement a *strategy*. Since this is a conflict between us and at least one other thinking person, who may also have a plan of action, our *strategy* (and *tactics*) must be adaptable and flexible to what is surely a changing environment.

Tactic – Method used to achieve a Strategy
This is how the battle is fought and where the remaining *Preparatory Considerations* are seen. Those are: *Maneuvers* (avoid the danger); *Targets* (openings on us and an opponent); *Natural Weapons* (ours and the opponents); *Natural Defenses* (ways we and an opponent can protect ourselves). In Kenpo, these are learned in the self-defense techniques.

I would add *Posture*, especially starting posture, to this list as it is different than *Position* and expand *Natural Weapons* to include any weapon, natural or not, and emphasize *Natural Defenses* using the environment around us, presuming a no rules environment.

If our scenario is evolving into a fight, then our body posture should be such as to accomplish several things. These include communicating to our adversary, and any bystanders/witnesses, that we do not want any trouble and that we are trying to avoid this physical confrontation.

This is done from a posture that looks relaxed and non-threatening but is still prepared to move and fight. I call it the "let's not fight," or, "I don't want to fight," posture in self-defense training. Standing naturally with the feet slightly staggered and hands up palms forward does this.

This is essentially a fighting stance because we are positioned to defend or attack but an opponent or onlookers (i.e. future witnesses) can think and if needed say later that we did not want to fight, from how they observed us standing. An attacker would also most likely be surprised by the capability contained within this posture, should they attack.

Two valuable books relating to this subject and a must read for martial artists are "The Art of War" by Sun Tzu and "The Book of 5 Rings" by Myamoto Musashi. Here is a summary:

"The Art of War" by Sun Tzu was written during the Warring States period in China, possibly earlier but pre-BC (BCE). It contains 13 Chapters on the Strategy and Tactics of warfare. This is a summary but read the book to more fully grasp these concepts.

1) *Laying Plans/5 Fundamental Strategies*. 1) The Way - have a moral cause; 2) Nature or Seasons; 3) Terrain or Environment; 4) Leadership; 5) Discipline.
2) *Waging War/Planning:* The economics and commitment to winning.
3) *Attack by Stratagem/Plan of Attack*: Strength in unity along with five ingredients to succeed in war (Attack, Strategy, Alliances, Army, Cities).
4) *Tactical Dispositions/Positioning*: Defending positions and how to recognize opportunities.
5) *Energy/Directing*: Creativity and timing while progressing towards victory.
6) *Weak Points & Strengths/Illusion*: Opportunities and openings caused by relative weaknesses in your opponent.
7) *Maneuvering/Engaging the Force*: The dangers of direct conflict and how to win when forced.
8) *Variation in Tactics/Nine Variations*: The need for flexibility in your responses as circumstances change.
9) *The Army or Force Moving/Marching*: Analyzing different situations.
10) *Terrain/Situational Positioning*: 5 things needed to calculate a plan of action; Mission, Climate, Ground, Leadership, Method.

11) *The Nine Situations/Nine Terrains*: Dispersive (fighting in your own territory), Light (no hazards), Contentious (fighting in opponent's territory), Open Ground (traversable), Focal (intersecting more than one territory), Serious (deep in opponent's territory), Heavy (lots of hazards), Entrapping (small routes out), Desperate (where you must fight).

12) *The Attack by Fire/Fiery Attack*: Weapons suited to the environment along with the five targets, five types of attack, and appropriate responses to those attacks.

13) *Use of Spies/Intelligence Gathering*: Developing useful information sources and managing them.

"The Book of 5 Rings" is by a famous Samurai Warrior in Japan during the 1600's named Miyamoto Musashi. This is a summary of his book but read the entire book to more fully grasp these concepts. The 5 Rings or Books:

1) The Book of Earth discusses preparation, like the building of a house.
2) The Book of Water discusses technique and fundamental principles.
3) The Book of Fire covers the heat of battle.
4) The Book of Wind discusses other styles of fighting.
5) The Book of the Void looks at the mind and moving without thought.

POSTURE

Posture is critically linked to balance and how the body is aligned for coordinated and powerful movement. For the martial artist, an aligned posture is the vital preparatory ingredient that gives the opportunity for effective offensive and defensive movements. The study of *Posture* can take the two major forms of *Static* and *Active*, i.e., *Dynamic Posture*.

Static Posture refers to body positions that are used while stationary although still containing dynamic capabilities. These postures build strength in the body while helping develop a feel for balance and leverage and are often held while learning individual basics in traditional training.

The horse stance is an example of a well thought out, perfectly balanced and elegant static posture. From the side, a plum line through the body starts from the center of the feet (Ki1), up the ankles, thru the hips and dantien, along the ribs (hands at Sp21), past the shoulders and chest, then ears, and up to the Bai Hui (GV20) or highest head point.

In traditional Karate and Kung Fu styles beginners especially spend a lot of time in this training horse stance, often practicing upper body basics. Besides providing a balanced bi-lateral practice position this posture builds whole-body strength by pre-loading major and many minor muscle groups.

The Neutral Bow fighting stance in Kenpo is similar to a Boxer's stance and an example of a static fighting posture with active and dynamic movement plus acceleration stored as "potential energy" for use as needed. An old Kenpo metaphor describes it as a flame that only burns if touched, illustrated in the original *International Karate Championships* patch that competitors received.

In either the horse or fighting stance, body parts are stacked vertically above each other giving structural integrity for flexible, controlled, powerful movement. With this mental understanding firmly engrained the brain then needs to let go so balanced movement can just happen and different applications developed.

Inanimate Object Posture Analogy:
Looking at any inanimate static object like a table, chair, or anything without a brain, the observation can be made of perfect posture with the object never falling over or losing its balance without outside interference. As obvious as this sounds much can be learned about posture and balance from observing physically stable inanimate objects.

The brain in people allows for mental and physical distractions to interfere with coordinating the 206 bones, over 360 joints, and more than 600 muscles in the body. This is too complicated for thought so it is best to remove the mind from the process and just be correct, yet inanimate, in our posture. Like Bruce Lee's famous *Enter the Dragon* movie line to his student, "Don't think, feeeeel."

Active (Dynamic) Posture is where the body transitions in place and/or on the ground with footwork for offensive and defensive applications to pre-load the body, feint an action, or draw an attack to counter, or just react to something unexpected.

A spinning Top can illustrate how balance is maintained while dynamically moving and turning. Take an old-fashioned Top and spin it to notice the peak of the Top (top of the Top) is directly above the base tip on the floor (bottom of the Top) while the Tops middle spins in place with perfect balance. This can also be seen by flicking a coin on its side causing it to spin on a tabletop.

Standing upright, we are akin to that Top with our head the top of our Top, our feet the base of our Top, with our shoulders and hips as the middle. Proper alignment allows for efficient and balanced turning, twisting, or moving in any direction. All of this happens dynamically in concert with mental intention to help give any movement optimal effectiveness.

Note that this top, bottom, middle concept aligned for balance and movement does not change with a different style or sports posture. This then brings height, width, and depth zones/dimensions into the analysis where one type of balanced posture can evolve, transition, adjust to another depending on the use.

A *height adjustment* involves moving up and down, commonly referred to as "changing levels" in grappling. For the striker like a boxer this would be ducking or bobbing and weaving and for grapplers it is a preparatory posture for shooting in or defending against a shot.

It is also used to feint or fake to draw a desired response from an opponent. In either case the body does not lean but drops straight down before any major shift in the weight or acceleration takes place. An important balance detail when adjusting the height down with the head upright is that one heel should be lifted higher off the ground the lower you go as a counterbalance, as done in the Kenpo *Wide Kneel Stance*. Grapplers (and Football players) tilt their shoulders forward with hips moving back to counterbalance when changing heights.

A *width adjustment* is commonly used in boxing to slip left and right but can also involve stepping from side to side or turning the shoulders and hips. Turning the shoulders and hips narrows the width and, in the process, elongates the depth.

A *depth adjustment* involves shifting the body forwards and backwards, with the feet and/or head moving in and out of range, like a mongoose fighting a cobra. This is done to draw an attack or to vary timing and break rhythm to setup an attack.

A common Muay Thai kickboxing posture has the hips slightly forward which keeps the head up and back allowing for greater vision and distance. It also preloads the hip flexors for acceleration to begin a wave of energy that often culminates in a powerful kick.

The common grappling posture has the hips pushed the hips back slightly, keeping the lower torso and legs away from an opponent, as the upper body is more strongly aligned to resist whole body pressure from the front. It also preloads the legs to jump back for sprawling or drive forward for takedowns.

Wrestlers do a more exaggerated version of this hips back posture, since they are not getting punched in the face, with the lesser version done more by MMA fighters especially when at close range.

In summary, static and active postures are done in combination so when engaged in martial arts they are dynamically changing to reflect the situation presented. The body is constantly in flux to setup whatever our intention is or to neutralize what our opponent is doing or has tried to do all the while trying to maintain a balanced posture.

BALANCE

Balance is essential for generating force as it supports the leverage and accelerated explosive power needed in martial arts. Without it the effectiveness of applied movement becomes difficult or even impossible, as would the ability to adjust the feet and body to avoid attack.

Gravity's effect on an unbalanced position is relentless and shows quickly by forcing rapid posture and foot adjustments to regain any loss of balance. This close interaction between balance and gravity is important since in a weightless environment balance cannot be attained and related potential force not generated or applied.

The result of striking if in space, weightless, would be weapons and targets pushing away from each other as the penetrating leverage of gravity supported back-up mass would be missing. Balance simply stated then is how we apply the earth's gravity while observing and using it to destabilize an opponent.

The three main body sections of static balance are the center of the body (dantien in TCM, centroid in Physics), the structural alignment of the torso and head (posture) stacked above that centerline, and a dynamic connection to the ground below through the legs and feet (traction). Maintaining this balance while moving involves counterbalance and other factors.

For martial arts these can be thought of from the two perspectives of our own balance and that of an opponent's. These dual factors add layers of sophistication to this subject and makes balance a critical concept for a martial artist to appreciate, understand, develop, and improve upon.

Leaving aside a description of the physiological mechanisms that the ears, eyes, and proprioception use to help us to feel and adjust our balance, this discussion presumes those components are functioning properly, so balance is evaluated here from the anatomical structure perspective.

Balance is *rooted* on the ground but felt in the body center with an aligned posture above and below with an understanding best started with our own balance. Once understood, then an opponent's balance can be read, felt, and controlled along six major bodylines individually or in combination to disrupt posture and position.

Controlling Our Own Balance
Presuming feet on the ground our anatomical center is located between our navel and pubic bone and between the front and backsides of our body, i.e. dantien.

To find it, draw three imaginary lines through the body intersecting below the navel at the coronal, sagittal, and transverse planes (See *Centerline* in Terminology chapter). The point inside where these three lines intersect is our body center for balance, power, and force. In Physics this is the centroid of an object, whether animate or inanimate.

Any activity that requires balance whether standing on one foot, both feet, or on both hands, demands we feel and control this center area while adjusting our body around it to maintain that balance. Much concentration and effort are given throughout life starting at the beginning to find this center and control our balance.

A baby starts lying flat on their stomachs, works up to the knees, then stands on the feet, walks, and eventually runs. *Counterbalance* is discovered and refined through this process with hip and opposite shoulder coordination becoming neurologically hardwired as our natural gait.

A baby should become comfortable with each step of this counterbalancing process before moving onto the next one. This allows for less conscious thought over time at each stage of movement as we develop a sense of balance. Some have a more natural or innate feel for their balance but anyone without a limiting disability can develop and improve upon it from where they start.

Posture is the next critical element of *balance* as the structure needs to be stacked above the center and down to the earth in a straight line. The upright standing posture of a martial artist is done with the knees bent and buttocks tucked slightly forward, to take the arch out of the sacrum and preload the hip flexors for forward movement.

The spinal vertebrae are stacked one above the other using the muscular structure for stability with the head sitting balanced on top and in control of the whole structure.

A Tai Chi visual describes the spines vertebral alignment as "a string of pearls hanging down from heaven." The head is lifted towards heaven (yang) with the feet are rooted on earth (yin) with the body naturally extended and comfortably supported in between and without tension.

The three main TCM points above the feet that align vertically are CV4 in the center of the dantien, CV17 in the center of the sternum, and GV20 at the top of the head (see *Pressure Point* chapter in the *Body*). These three also correspond to Chakras used in that system of energetics.

The "String of Pearls" visual leaves us with a lifted, erect, and balanced posture prepared for athletic movement, including applying powerful martial art moves individually or in combination.

Note: Even Jello has a center so the *intention* behind the visual should not be lost in the analysis relating to the animate human body, at least for martial arts use.

With good posture stacked above the body center understood, controlling balance then becomes the legs' ability to support the body weight while standing or actively moving. The foot to ground connection is the next important piece to understand in this balance equation.

Four main concepts for feeling how the bottoms of the feet connect and interact with the ground come from the *Western Anatomical Model*, the *Movement Athletes Model*, the *Eastern Energetics Model*, and the *Chinese Martial Arts Model*. Training builds this connection with the legs ability to move with dynamic structural leverage.

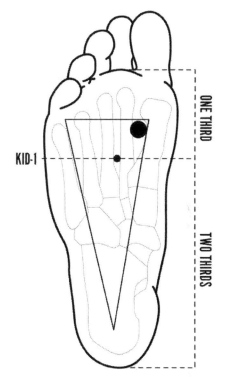

The *Western Anatomical Model* analysis of foot anatomy observes three high (or low) points on the bottoms of each foot. The bottom of heel (calcaneus), ball of foot at the big toe (distal 1st metatarsal bone), and little toe ball (distal 5th metatarsal bone).

If connected with lines these form an Isosceles triangle (2 equal sides with 2 equal angles) giving us a visual of a stable balanced structure connected to the ground.

The *Movement Athletes Model* used by dancers, yoga enthusiasts, and sprinters puts the weight to the inside ball of the foot, on the big toe side (black dot on illustration). Putting the weight at this point shifts the knees and inner thighs slightly inwards, moving the legs connection closer to our physical center, where explosive muscle groups can be more easily engaged. This contraction around the core provides powerful, fast, and efficient movement potential.

The *Eastern Energetics Model* recognizes the acupuncture point Kidney 1 (KID-1 on foot image) as the middle balance point under the foot, and the lowest energetic point on the body (where yin anchors to earth). On the opposite end GV20 (Bai Hui) on top of the head is the highest point (where yang lifts towards heaven).

Ki1 is on the sole of the foot between the second and third metatarsals approximately one-third between the base of the second toe and heel. It is in a depression formed when the toes are lifted, and the ball of the foot is pressed onto the floor. This is the center balance point of the foot and contained within the previously described triangle.

Note: This point has its equal on the palms of the hand at *P8 / Lao Gong / Palace of Toil*, where the middle fingertip rests when you make a fist, which is also the energetic center of most hand shapes such as a palm strike, handsword, etc. If walking on our hands this would be the balance center on each hand. This palm center is also the focus for methods that train to push Qi out through the hands, as practiced in Qi Gong, and where most hand weapon shapes form around.

The *Chinese Martial Art Model* used by *Internal* styles like Tai Chi imagines roots growing from the bottoms of the feet into the ground. This reinforces balance by connecting the brain finitely to the toes and entire bottom foot structure to the ground. This is developed slowly and over time as this visual rooting goes deeper into the ground making for an ever deepening and stable connection.

Any or all these visuals can help the mind understand and reinforce the foot to ground connection better. Experiment and find what works for you or come up with your own concept so balance can be better understood and reinforced intellectually, visually, and physically.

Once intellectual comprehension and physical adjustment has taken place, let it go and feel balance without conscious thought. The good news with human balance is that we have a brain to analyze and understand, and the bad news is that we have a brain that can get in the way.

As discussed under *Posture*, inanimate objects can teach us in this regard as they have no difficulty maintaining balance. A table will not suddenly fall over yet even mild outside interference, or a mental distraction, can easily make a person lose their balance.

Since balance must shift to travel, the next component is how the foot/feet pivot(s) on the ground. Using the most effective pivot(s) to accomplish the task of creating distance, closing distance, maintaining proper foot width, etc., is an important and often under-appreciated detail in martial arts.

The two main pivot points on the bottoms of each foot are the heel and ball, although the big toe can be used with less weight. With both feet on the ground the four main pivot point combinations then are right heel/left heel, right ball/left ball, right ball/left heel, or left ball/right heel (see *Basics* in the *Body*).

This balance discussion started with the center of the body and then stacked the body above that center before analyzing this foot connection with the ground. These components of a concept like balance can be thought of and explained in any order but the components are the same regardless.

Controlling an Opponent's Balance
By understanding our own balance, we are better able to understand other people's balance as we are all limited by the same gravity. There are four major *Awareness Keys* in observing an opponent's balance that can be affected along six major *Balance Lines*.

The four *Awareness Keys* are *Foot Alignment, Posture, Leg Weight Distribution,* and *Foot Area Distribution.* Timing and an understanding of how to compound multiple balance disruptions to control an opponent should also be understood and practiced, i.e., *Range Manipulation* in Kenpo.

Foot Alignment is important because how the attacker places and turns his feet will affect what he can do and determine the most effective angles to attack and break his balance. In Kenpo we refer to this as the strong line / weak line dynamic, which can be analyzed using 8 points on a clock.

The Fighting Stance figure below on the left has 12 to 6 as the strongest line with approximately 3 to 9 as the weakest. The Horse Stance figure on the right is strongest from 3 to 9 and weakest 12 to 6. The weakest balance line then goes perpendicular to the foot alignment with the strongest line parallel with that alignment.

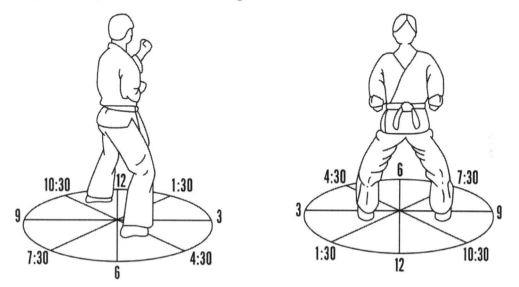

Posture refers to whether an opponent is standing straight, bent over, turned or square, all of which can reveal his intentions by observing the loading of his body for acceleration and power. See *Posture*.

Leg Weight Distribution is the committed body weight on one leg or the other. It can be evenly distributed all on either foot or in various amounts between the two feet, and it can be dynamically shifting between the legs.

Recognizing tendencies and habits or causing predictable weight transfers and adjustment steps can become an advantage as an opponent telegraphs their intention, becoming vulnerable during this time.

Foot Area Distribution observes how weight is shifted onto various parts of the feet and in what proportions or the rate of shifting as this dynamic can be manipulated or be voluntarily in flux. It also relates to the foot to ground connection, heel and toe weight distribution, and pivoting.

Using clock angles while <u>standing on the right foot as a baseline</u>, eight (8) points or angles can be disrupted causing an unbalanced weight shift where the body center shifts, and/or the body leans, and/or the opposite foot takes an adjustment step, and/or the same foot hops, and/or the hand(s) reach for support to grab or brace from falling. These are caused by:

1) *Shifting their weight straight forward onto toes* (Fist of Aggression); to 12 from right foot baseline.

2) *Shifting their weight forward onto front (little toe side) outside of foot* (Taming the Fist); to 1:30 from right foot baseline.

3) *Shifting their weight sideways onto outside edge of foot* (Spiralling Wrist); to 3 from a right foot baseline.

4) *Shifting their weight back onto outside edge of heel* by pushing (Tripping Leg) or pulling (Turn of Fate); to 4:30 from a right foot baseline.

5) *Shifting their weight straight back onto back edge of heel* (Pursuing Panther); to 6 from a right foot baseline.

6) *Shifting their weight back onto inside foot edge* (The Nutcracker); to 7:30 from a right foot baseline.

7) *Shifting their weight sideways to inside foot edge* (Untwirling Pendulum); to 9 from a right foot baseline.

8) *Shifting their weight forward onto front big toe side inside* (Triggered Palm); to 10:30 from a right foot baseline.

This analysis can also be seen standing on the left foot or both feet where the *strong line* is the most difficult to disrupt. It can be used individually or compounded into follow up disruptions like pushing someone's weight back then pulling it forward (Blinding Vice), etc.

Timing is used to see and feel the right moment to use the best balance disruption method before the opportunity is lost. An athletic opponent, and especially a trained person, will recover balance quickly so an adept practitioner takes their balance and doesn't allow them to have it back until the goal is accomplished.

Balance Lines describe six (6) horizontal lines on the human structure using anatomical reference points near joints where movement takes place. These can be observed, adjusted, or manipulated to affect balance.

The study of push-hands in Chinese martial arts or any grappling style like Judo, Jiu Jitsu, and Wrestling all give an immediate feel for our own and another person's balance, and how difficult it is to control. A cooperative effort like partner dancing is another useful way to develop a feel for another person's balance when moving on the feet.

In Kenpo, this controlling of another person's balance is called *Range Manipulation or* carrying our opponent. It is an advanced concept that underlies much of the effectiveness of Kenpo technique combinations. Kenpo practitioners should search for this in every technique to understand and practice this important range of fighting. Standing naturally with arms by the side the six (6) Balance Lines are:

1) Temple-to-Temple line (determines head position)
2) Shoulder-to-Shoulder line (determines shoulder position)
3) Waist-to-Waist/Elbow-to-Elbow line (determines upper torso position)
4) Hip-to-Hip/Wrist-to-Wrist line (determines body center position)
5) Knee-to-Knee line (determines leg position)
6) Ankle-to-Ankle line (determines foot placement)

Note: The elbow-to-elbow and wrist-to-wrist lines can also be considered independent of the waist and hip lines since the arms range of motion is considerable and can be used separate from those other lines

Once foot alignment, posture, weight transfer, and distribution are seen then attacking one or more of these balance lines are more effectively used and can be applied from any position.

The **Temple-to-Temple** line goes through the eyes so pushing, pulling, or striking to move the head on this target line disrupts equilibrium by shifting the body at the neck. This causes a point of imbalance as the head can be moved around to any of 360° with the body following the head, and possibly causing neck damage.

Examples: Against a front bear hug with arms free their left temple is struck as our other hand pulls their head sideways with a step sideways outside their foot (Tripping Leg) or striking chin and opposite sides temple simultaneously to tweak the neck (Destructive Gift).

The **Shoulder-to-Shoulder** line goes across the upper chest and back so pushing, pulling, or striking one or both shoulders can disrupt balance and change their posture.

Examples: This can be done by turning (Turn of Fate) or tipping (Spiralling Wrist) them. If able to get behind an opponent, then his two shoulders can be grabbed, and his weight shifted back onto both heels for follow-up strikes and body manipulations (Backbreaker).

The **Waist-to-Waist/Elbow-to-Elbow** line goes through the body just above the top of the hip bones or waist so pushing, pulling, striking one side or both, and/or manipulating an elbow can affect an opponent's balance. The waist includes the side, front, and back where it can greatly affect upper body movement.

Example: Attacking the waist directly can move the upper body sideways (Reversing Fist), attacking the stomach can cause it to bend forward (Grabbing Hair), or a low spine attack causing it to arch backwards (Backbreaker). With the elbow, bending (Triggered Palm) or hyper-extending (Conquering Arm) can also be used to manipulate.

The **Hip-to-Hip/Wrist-to-Wrist** line travels through the lower hips to top of the legs and groin so pushing, pulling, or striking on one side or both can affect balance and posture, and/or manipulating the wrist.

Examples: This line is like the waist line but affects the lower body more so affecting the hips (Destructive Gift), groin (Hooking Arms), and tailbone (Hidden Hand) are directly connected to the legs. The wrist can also be used to manipulate the weight (Crossing Grab).

The **Knee-to-Knee** line occurs at the knee joint in any direction where it can be manipulated.

Examples: These can happen inside (Entangled Arm B), outside (Hand & Shield), in front (Twins of Aggression), or to the rear/back of the knee (Buckling the Leg) where it can buckle, hyper-extend, and/or shift weight, all of which disrupts balance.

The **Ankle-to-Ankle** line occurs at the ankle joint and feet.

Examples: This line can be swept (Untwirling Pendulum), struck or trapped (Broken Kneel), picked up (Nutcracker), or manipulated (Brushing the Club) at different angles to trip, takedown, or widen a base to disrupt their balance.

These six (6) *Balance Lines* can also be compounded using combinations and progressive sequences to break down an opponent.

Examples: Lifting the wrist as the head is pushed down affects all the lines (Delayed Hand). Pulling the wrist can also affect the elbow (Cross of Destruction), pushing the temple and shoulder together can manipulate posture (Thundering Fists), pressing into the knee while pulling the foot can be used to takedown (Straddling the Leg), buckling the knee can expose the ankle (Evading the Club), etc.

These are used to move an opponent's center, narrow or widen his base, cause imbalance, and they overlap the *Dimensional Zone* concept covered later. This all greatly increases technique effectiveness and can bring a practitioner to another level.

FOCUS

For this discussion *Focus* refers to our mind fully concentrated with our eyes engaged. The available visual field is a major factor, with posture and distance also playing a valuable role, as do controlling the breath, and opening the eyes wide as they 'spot' or re-spot a target after losing sight.

Focus involves a lack of distraction in our mind while using our eyes to relay changes so our brain can evaluate, interpret, and adapt to stimulus. Aside from the realities of a dangerous situation, causing a Sympathetic Nervous System or Stress Response that may include tunnel vision, there are two focus concepts using the eyes discussed by Ed Parker in his writings and teachings. Those are *White Dot Focus* and *Black Dot Focus*.

The standard Kenpo explanation is that a traditional, or hard linear martial art style, uses the white dot on a black background to draw the focus of the eyes for maximum mental and physical focus, but has less awareness of the black space around it. This tends to ignore, at least for that moment, potential threats around the white dot or follow up targets that are contained in the black background area.

Ed Parker saw this flaw and espoused a concept he termed *Black Dot Focus* that visualizes a black dot on a white background, allowing for not only focused attention to the black dot but for more awareness of the white background that surrounds it.

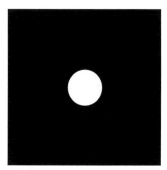

The reality of looking at the identically sized images illustrated here is that the mind can be convinced either image represents either perspective. The mind can focus on the black dot in the white space or white dot in the black background with or without awareness to the surrounding space, or even decide the dot is in the background. Regardless of our interpretation the important thing to note is that there are these two perspectives, which are also contained in the yin/yang symbol.

It is useful on many occasions to get lost in the white dot to the detriment of the black background as with brick breaking, hitting a baseball, or studying for an exam. When it comes to fighting the *Black Dot Focus* concept is useful to help keep an awareness of the entire visual field and situation, and perhaps multiple threats that may exist.

We can all observe ourselves moving into and out of both types of focus. In martial arts a total awareness of an attacker's posture and position *(Black Dot Focus)*, with moments of pinpoint focus while striking a target *(White Dot Focus)*. In addition, an attacker with a weapon draws the most attention as the weapon especially becomes the primary focus.

Researchers who study and practice optimizing eye utilization say there are 5 focus abilities (source: Flashfocus.net). Those are:

Dynamic Visual Acuity (DVA): The eyes ability to accurately follow a moving object. This is an essential skill in car racing, hitting a baseball, or tracking a punch or kick. This is dynamic *White Dot Focus*.

Momentary Vision: An ability to quickly identify an object as it enters your range of vision. In sports, this skill may be important for quickly spotting movement like a wide receiver in football turning to pick up the ball already in flight, or an incoming strike that is seen late. This is moving from *Black Dot Focus* to *White Dot Focus*.

Eye Movement: How the eyes rapidly shift focus between more than one object. This is done when reading, driving, or fighting multiple moving opponents. This is dynamic alternating of *White* and *Black Dot Focus*.

Peripheral Vision: This allows us to spot objects in the area outside our central vision. This skill can be helpful in tracking new movements around a center point or be used as a feint. This is *Black Dot Focus*.

Hand-Eye Coordination (HEC): Helps judge distance and timing using our eyes to then respond by accurately using our hands within the context of our body. These reactions are essential in daily life not to mention in sports and especially in fighting. This is a moving White Dot Focus.

The conclusion is that we cannot avoid moving in and out of both Black Dot and White Dot focus whether in our day-to-day life or while engaged in sports or fighting. Awareness of this can lead us to practice more effectively and is an area where sport fighting provides real-life experience in this eye focus development for the martial artist.

SPEED

For most, speed refers to how fast movement occurs, but Kenpo founder Ed Parker defined three types of speed for the martial artist. The first two, *Perceptual Speed* and *Mental Speed* are about reaction time, with the third *Physical Speed* as response time.

Perceptual Speed is how long it takes to recognize and evaluate a situation, assess a potential or real threat while gaining awareness of the environment. This can preempt needing to use martial art skills by avoiding the perceived threat or provide an awareness advantage when entering into an environment perceived to be threatening.

Observing attitudes and postures, noticing how many people pose a threat, weapons they may have, escape routes, environmental objects available, etc. This is seeing a hungry tiger before it sees you.

Mental Speed is how fast situations are assessed once a threat has been detected and a plan of action is developed. Once the hungry tiger is seen and perhaps sees you the mental decision-making process could involve running away, bluffing, fighting, etc.

This is a place where training and life experience is the most valuable, so if we were trained in how to deal with a hungry tiger, we would revert to that training automatically, hopefully with confidence and decisiveness. This minimizes an adrenaline filled decision-making process that can save time, confusion, and mistakes.

Physical Speed is how fast the body moves to execute a chosen response. In the case of the hungry tiger, maybe we don't move at all, or suddenly and quickly to nearby safety, or we grab a weapon to help us fight the tiger. If the tiger leaps, we have no choice but to react quickly to try and avoid the danger.

Sometimes called "quick reflexes" this type of speed fits the standard definition of what most people think of as speed since it's how fast the body mass reacts to stimulus and physically moves. This process of moving rapidly can be explained by *muscle twitch, acceleration,* and *body alignment*.

Muscle twitch is made up of *slow* and *fast-twitch muscle fibers*. The *slow-twitch* fibers can contract for extended periods of time but do not generate much force, whereas the *fast-twitch* fibers contract quickly and powerfully but fatigue easily. Some people are lightning fast, and some people are granite strong with most falling in between or alternating.

Fast-twitch fibers are improved with speed drills and exercises that require explosive quick movements. *Slow-twitch* fibers are improved with strength building exercises for muscular endurance. A holistic approach is taken in martial arts to develop both capabilities.

Acceleration is a main component of this type of speed to help build *power* and generate *force*. Acceleration is an increasing change in speed over time of which there are two types.

First is to move faster or gain speed through a *linear* or straight path with the second following a *circular* or arced path. The arced path can get smaller (centripetal energy) or larger (centrifugal energy) as it moves towards a target. This can move through one target to reaccelerate towards another target moving small to large (Triggered Palm) or large to small (Snapping Arm) for example.

Body Alignment is when the component parts of the body are put into a position to generate movement most efficiently and effectively. This generally requires instruction as the untrained eye cannot know what it does not know and even with training it is difficult to see ourselves objectively, even on video.

With quality instruction correct muscle and structural memory becomes ingrained in the body to where incorrect movement no longer feels "normal" as was perceived previously before this awareness was attained. With good structural habits over time we can get the most speed, efficiency, and effectiveness from our movement while optimizing power and preventing injury.

POWER

Philosophically speaking there are several types of power such as mental, financial, emotional, power of personality, etc. All are "powerful" concepts of *Power* with the discussion here and commonly in martial arts relating to physical power. This type of *power* can be measured through the science of Physics.

However, *Power* is a relative concept that can be applied on many levels as it relates to human physical interaction and as practiced in martial arts where it can become more complicated, or perhaps more sophisticated. Even though a strong man is more powerful than a weak man he is not more powerful than a car which is not more powerful than a hurricane.

Within the human structure these strong and weak relationships also exist so even though one person's body may be stronger than another person's body there are many weapons on a weaker person that can overwhelm targets on a stronger person.

A weaker person's accelerated handsword for example may be more powerful than a stronger person's trachea (Hidden Hand) or a weaker person's arm may be more powerful than a stronger person's finger (Gripping Wrist).

One of the great efficiencies, equalizers, and confidence builders in martial arts is in gaining this knowledge of the existence of the many power to resistance mismatches that exist in the human structure relative to another human structure.

For martial arts purposes *Power* refers to how much force is needed to have an effect and to what degree on a target, or the power a weapon generates relative to the target utilizing various *Point of Contact Variables* (See Motion & Movement).

A method's effectiveness is optimized through this weapon/target dynamic with technique, alignment, intention, focus, effort, breath, timing, acceleration, velocity, leverage, back-up mass, cardiovascular and muscular endurance, etc. all as factors.

Unifying these concepts and principles into single or combination movements, whether for martial arts or another physical activity, allows for the generation of maximum focused, directed and regulated force relative to a resistance that is intended or needed to accomplish a task.

This concept of *Power* transcends martial arts and can be seen in other chapters within this book series. Read the *Vocabulary & Terminology* section definitions in this book for *Acceleration - Back Up Mass - Energy (Kinetic & Potential) - Force - Inertia - Power - Explosiveness - Momentum - Point of Contact Variables - Muscle Spindle Cell (MSC) - Golgi Tendon Organ (GTO)*. Also see the *Pressure Point* and *Basics* chapters in the *Body*.

DIRECTIONS & ANGLES

Directions refer to where the intention of the physical body is aimed. **Angles** define the path followed to move in a direction. Both require physiological and mental perspective to know how those *Directions* and *Angles* can be seen by the body.

The most obvious way is through the eyes but in martial arts what the weapon sees is also important as they have their own valuable perspective/viewpoint. The directions and angles seen from the perspective of the hands and feet are invaluable in determining available targets, all while the eyes provide the larger environmental picture.

DIRECTIONS

These can have more than one reference or meaning by using the *Clock Concept* with its horizontal references on the floor and vertical references on a wall, both using 8 major directions of attack and defense for analysis purposes.

This visual can also be projected in the mind to include a directional sphere that we are all inside where diagonals become interlocked three-dimensionally with those horizontal and vertical images. Together these help us not only analyze attack and defense from those major directions but any degree within a $360°^2$ sphere, accounting for every possible direction.

The horizontal floor reference is especially useful for beginners, with intermediate students able to benefit more by adding the vertical reference. Advanced practitioners can start to relate the three-dimensional sphere concept after fully grasping the other two.

To understand the horizontal (floor) reference, picture yourself standing in the middle of a large clock. Directly in front is the 12 o'clock reference point. Moving with knowledge of where other points exist on the clock becomes helpful in analyzing, relating, understanding, and remembering the directional focus of movement more thoroughly. The vertical (wall) reference sees the high point in front at 12 and the low at 6, with 3 on the right and 9 on the left.

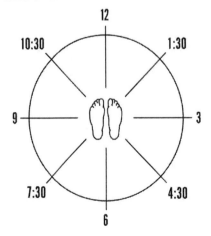 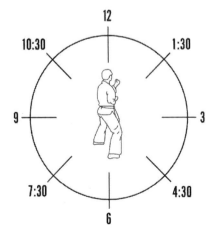

The three-dimensional sphere concept contains 360° x 360°, or 360°². This huge increase in the amount of attack and defense directions is needed for a deeper understanding of movement with flexibility as to how and where attack and defense can be applied.

Another way to look at the *Clock Concept* is to understand possible directions and angles using mathematics. Geometric symbols like "plus +," "minus –," and "times x" can describe directions or different angles to analyze and that can relate to movement, and not even getting into compounding actions.

ANGLES
In martial arts, angles are used to evaluate body positioning for attack and defense. These are determined and recognized moving in space, relating to joints, applied onto body parts, and/or how they relate to an entire body.

Angles have three components: The *Vertex* is the corner, the *Arms* are the two straight sides stemming from the *Vertex*, and the *Angle* is the gap between the *Arms*. Together they make for six distinct types of angles.

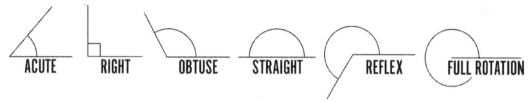

ACUTE　　RIGHT　　OBTUSE　　STRAIGHT　　REFLEX　　FULL ROTATION

Martial arts use every piece of this angle equation. For example, the elbow *vertex* can hinge open or closed to strike (acute, right, obtuse, straight), or be closed to hook or hinge forward (reflex, full rotation). It can also be used statically bent (acute) applying the sharp outside tip or inside crease.

The *arms* of these angles can also be utilized for blocking, striking, or checking, and can move in all directions. Understanding different angle types can be a useful towards gaining insight into fighting techniques.

The dynamic of human body movement, whether in the air or interacting with another person, can be very fluid making all angles and their components potentially always in flux. Setting aside the importance of structural alignment they can be looked at and understood individually.

Acute Angles are less than 90° and in the *Clock Concept* these 45° angles define each major direction of attack and defense. Looking at the elbow this shape can be used to strike out with the tip (Fist of Aggression) or choke using the inside crease (Turn of Fate).

Right Angles are at 90° where two perpendicular lines intersect to form a corner or square, as in a cross-body check (Sweeping the Leg). This angle is also seen in foot maneuver practice as the turn is done at 90° angles.

Obtuse Angles are greater than 90° but less than 180°. This *arms* angle shape can be used traveling away from the centerline as a backknuckle strike (Alternating Fist) or inward as a round punch (Darting Fist).

Straight Angles are when the two arms are in alignment with no angle arc between so is said to be at 180º. Extending an arm or leg completely forms this shape at the point of contact whether applied as a linear path of motion straight punch (Crossing Fist) or a circular paths roundhouse kick (Broken Kneel).

Reflex Angles are greater than 180º but less than 270º and are essentially the backside of an obtuse angle. An outward hook kick forms this shape and travels through this angle (Rear Belt Grab) along with any overhead downward strike (Charging Tackle).

Full Rotation Angles describe movements that make a complete 360º circle with the arm (Wraparound) or leg (Defending Cross).

Discussions of angles are used extensively in Kenpo with Ed Parker coining many of the terms used in this section. His descriptions are in "parenthesis" with my own explanations included to expand or clarify.

ANGLE OF CANCELLATION – "A controlled angle that places an opponent in a precarious position, thus minimizing or even nullifying the use of his weapons." Neutralizing an opponent's options is done through body alignment (Reversing Fist), manipulation (Compulsive Kneel), or by direct aggressive force to a weapon (Securing the Club).

ANGLE OF CONTACT – This is the most effective angle to apply a weapon onto a target. This contact can occur at a 90º *Angle of Incidence* (Parting Arms) or diagonals that glance through a target (Raking Fist).

ANGLE OF DEFLECTION – The angle measured between the intended path of a weapon and its newly adjusted path after being moved by a block (Crossing Fist), inward/outward parry combo (Destructive Circles), or jamming a weapon (Rolling Fists).

ANGLE OF DELIVERY – "The position from which one's natural weapons may be executed with accuracy, efficiency, and effectiveness." This is the path of motion from *Point of Origin* to *Point of Destination* such as in a front snap kick to the groin (Delayed Hand) or an obscure elbow strike under the chin (Captured Arms), and not always a straight line as in a groin hammerfist followed by a nose backknuckle (Unrolling Crane).

ANGLE OF DEPARTURE – The most efficient and safest direction to take when exiting based upon relative positioning and as influenced by posture or weight distribution (Hooking Arms), the physical environment (Turning Windmills), or additional opponents (Training the Bears).

ANGLE OF DEVIATION / ADJUSTMENT – Where angular adjustments are made allowing for movement to a safer zone of defense (Returning the Club) or as positioned for a stronger offensive alignment (Triggered Palm).

ANGLE OF DISTURBANCE – "That angle created when a move is executed that does not necessarily injure but rather upsets an opponent's balance." It is used to change posture and direction (Falling Eagle).

ANGLE OF ENTRY – "Any degree, or path (angle) of approach, whether linear or circular in execution, it allows you or your opponent access to specific targets. This path of approach can be executed horizontally, diagonally or vertically from any direction."

This is what the weapon sees in finding the most efficient path to a target, such as the gap between an attackers two hands when attempting a wristlock (Entangled Arm A), or the diagonal path of a round kick into the groin (Evading the Club). This is the alignment before the angle of delivery is followed to the target. See *Line of Entry* to differentiate.

ANGLE OF INCIDENCE – "The 90° angle formed when a weapon strikes a target." This angle occurs at the point where a weapon meets a target (Clipping the Blade 1-2). See *Angle of Contact* to differentiate.

ANGLE OF NO RETURN – Body positioning where it becomes awkward and not practical to return along the same path, aka *Point of No Return*. The classic Kenpo example is where the hips rotate, the leg extends, and the weight drops to do a side thrust kick (*Buckling the Leg* base version) where it would be difficult and unnecessary to readjust the hips back to point of origin, making a front crossover step the logical exit maneuver.

ANGLE OF OBSCURITY – Blind spots or positions outside of the peripheral vision that, in Kenpo, covers *Zones of Obscurity* and *Obscure Zones*. The two main perspectives, or *viewpoints*, in this regard are the opponent's (Hidden Elbow) and ours (Twin Lapel Grab).

ANGLE OF PROTECTION – "The positioning of your body to give you maximum shield against anticipated strikes." (Hand and Shield)

ANGLE OF REDIRECTION – The degree of change made after a strike makes contact that is used to change paths towards a new target (Shielding Fingers).

Together, a side thrust kick to the back of a knee set up by an angle of deflection, followed by an angle of deviation/adjustment to step behind them into an angle of protection, before kicking from an angle of obscurity, following an angle of entry that tracks along an angle of delivery causing an angle of disturbance. This is applied at an angle of contact that could either glance thru causing an angle of redirection or be applied straight making for an angle of incidence that causes an angle of cancellation. This puts us at an angle of no return where we can follow the best angle of departure (Buckling the Leg).

Summary: Knowledge and analysis of these different angles is done to understand how to optimize our own technique and cancel an opponent's favorable angles. Comparing the shape and potential of angles and the components that make up this natural phenomenon can give insight into natures design and how we can use it more effectively and efficiently.

DISTANCE & TIMING

Distance and Timing are closely related in martial arts as it usually takes one to accomplish the other effectively on another person. These topics are viewed here from the self-defense and sport fighting perspectives.

DISTANCE
The travel distance between weapons and targets is referred to as *range* with the space between them commonly known as the *gap*. These are primarily seen through the *depth* dimension and are used to regulate space for attack and defense.

In a sport fight, the gap will generally increase and decrease allowing for different techniques to be within range. In street, this gap is best kept larger until a point of action forces it to close rapidly, and from where it may not open again until the fight is over. In either case, this gap is a extremely competitive contentious space where much of a fight takes place.

Offensively, the art of closing the gap is accomplished using various setup techniques, body reads, and disguised rhythm methods to take advantage of, and to create openings.

Defensively, to avoid being hit the gap can be increased to *Out-Of-Range* or decreased with three *In-Range* options, notwithstanding getting hit. Those three are to *jam* the weapon(s) at the source or just attack first, *block* or intercept/catch the weapon(s) with a more durable body part, or to *evade* the attacking weapon(s) by moving the target.

Ed Parker contributed *Stages of Range*, which I use here as a base for my own interpretation and observations. My explanation breaks range into *Range Depth Zones for Self-Defense*, i.e., street methods, and *Range Depth Zones for 1-1 Sport Fighting*, i.e., sparring. These two viewpoints are useful in that they overlap yet consider the uniqueness of each approach.

Range Depth Zones for Self Defense:
Out of Range – <u>Cannot</u> reach an aggressor and they <u>cannot</u> reach us. This term covers a full array of distances, from being just outside of *In-Range* to being in your car driving away from the conflict. In the self-defense context the goal is to stay out of a potential attacker's range, at least 3'-6' away, as you try to not engage.

In-Range – <u>Can</u> reach an aggressor and they <u>can</u> reach us, but we are not yet engaged. This dangerous place is where an aggressor could attack at any moment (i.e., "Sucker Punch"), making angling and body position crucial to an effective response. This range is inclusive of the next three as any of those are also *In-Range,* making it important to recognize which range(s) is/are threatening to change to a safer distance or our preferred range, or just attack first.

Contact Range – Touching the surface of an opponent's body or a limb, or they are touching us, whether striking a body surface or reaching out to connect and touch as in a gauge or check. The gap is often closed in this manner by touching a limb, the body, or even the head as a preliminary point of contact from where deeper contact and manipulation may evolve with varying elements of control over an opponent at this and each subsequent range.

Penetration Range – Accelerated weapons that hit with roughly 2"-3" of penetration, or that moves the target to that depth upon contact or is a combination of penetration and movement. This is accomplished through acceleration, leverage, weapon to target alignment, and of course intention (or bad intentions as it were).

Range Manipulation – Where the ability to control or move an opponent occurs. This can be done by pulling, pushing, striking, twisting, sweeping, bumping, or feinting to cause a voluntary position change. This is known in Kenpo as "carrying an opponent."

This range encompasses the closely related, or even synonymous, *Contact Manipulation, Control Manipulation,* and *Counter Manipulation* (see *Vocabulary and Terminology*).

This range especially benefits from knowledge and awareness of strong line vs weak line, weight transfer, balance, and angles that can defeat certain muscle groups. Drills, methods, and techniques that develop a feel for an opponent's center give opportunities to practice and gain the insight needed to apply this difficult and sophisticated range of fighting.

Range Depth Zones for 1-1 Sport Fighting / Sparring:
Since sport fighting is, by definition, an agreed upon and mutually engaged fight there are three primary ranges at work: *Striking, Clinch/Stand up Grappling,* and *Ground Grappling*. These would encompass the five *Range Depth Zones for Self-Defense*, but from the view of a "fair fight."

Some sport methods strive to dominate at one range of fighting. Boxers use their fists to punch but with grappling generally illegal and grapplers hold and maneuver with another person but with striking generally illegal. Muay Thai uses striking and stand-up grappling where MMA uses striking and ground fighting with some clinch work and "dirty boxing."

The best sport fighters, and strikers especially, are trained in controlling the gap between themselves and their opponent while moving between *In Range* and *Out of Range*. That is how an opponent is studied or felt and how his timing is figured out, and how he is set up for attack.

Striking Range – Impacting moves that cover distance while hitting primarily with the hands, arms, feet, and legs. The major concept applied is controlling the space or gap between opponents so that weapons have room to accelerate, impact, and penetrate. Striking sport styles include Boxing, Kickboxing, Sport Karate, and Tae Kwon Do.

The distance to or from a standup opponent could be 1½ steps away (Point Fighting range), 1 step away (Kickboxing range), or a ½ step away (Boxing range). These distances are used because the rules of those sports make them the most effective to achieve success in competition. See *Sport Fighting* chapter in the *Body*.

<u>Clinch or Stand-Up Grappling Range</u> – Holding, hugging, and grabbing primarily with the hands and arms, but also includes trips, sweeps, reaps, throws, or other takedowns with the legs, hips, and/or upper body.

Clinch or stand-up grappling sport styles include wrestling (Folkstyle, Freestyle, and especially Greco-Roman), Judo, Aikido, Chin Na, and Jiu Jitsu to a lesser degree. The major concept is to push, pull, hold, hook, grab, lock, beat up and wear down an opponent with the goal of controlling and manipulating their center of balance. This is done towards the sport goal of winning while minimizing our potential vulnerabilities.

<u>Ground Grappling Range</u> - Grabbing and controlling with the hands, arms, body, and legs, with fighters sitting, kneeling, or laying down. Also occurring is the generally temporary position where one combatant is down with the other standing.

In these methods fighters utilize theirs and an opponent's body along with the ground for compression, leverage, and pivoting. This is all done to control and wear down with the goal of pinning, submitting, or winning on points. Ground grappling sport styles include Wrestling, Jiu Jitsu, Judo, and Sambo.

A major concept in grappling is to eliminate space to control and make an opponent uncomfortable. Depending on the rules, competitors search for opportunities to manipulate, pin, suffocate, choke, joint lock, or cause discomfort to make an opponent give up (i.e., submit).

TIMING
The synchronization and coordination of basics to achieve the intended result, of which there are the two major definitions or perspectives of *Movement Timing* and *Application Timing*.

<u>Movement Timing</u> is the unification of *Mind* (understanding & insight) with *Body* (form & technique) and *Spirit* (enthusiasm & effort) where the body parts are coordinated to work together with the breath and mental intention. This definition is often developed practicing movements or patterns in the air (i.e., Sets, Forms, and Shadowboxing). This develops into what is referred to in martial arts as someone's "level of movement."

<u>Application Timing</u> is the reactive and reflexive interaction that takes place

with another person. Controlling the gap by effectively closing range to a target or position, by effectively reacting to an opponent's movement, or altering a moves cadence, rhythm, or tempo are all crucial aspects of timing whether for sport or street. The most effective moment used and acted upon is the essence of applying this concept of *timing*.

With that knowledge we can bait and wait then counter with a proactive reaction or pre-empt and attack before their effort is launched. Even though this awareness is important, it can only be taken advantage of with a knowledge of and utilization of "good timing."

An important sport-fighting tactic is to control the gap between combatants. Controlling the space effectively to use the range of fighting we prefer, or where we perceive the opponent to be weakest. The goal in striking is to hit and not get hit so this gap control makes that more possible.

Once controlled, moving to an opening with no obvious preliminary setup requires seeing or anticipating an opening to attack, and being close enough to reach it before defended. Whether we see a step, set-point, angle change, body rhythm, tic, weight shift, tendency, or notice/create a mental distraction, a breath, or even a blink, these can all be used as timing openings.

Taking advantage of these openings requires explosive, aggressive, and committed movement relentlessly applied with an intention towards victory. The flow of this is regulated and varied depending on other factors that include rhythm, broken rhythm, and tempo. These are the fakes and feints done to create openings.

Rhythm
This refers to a steady pace with an even and predictable cadence. For this purpose, we are trying to use *Rhythm* to read an opponent and lull him into a rhythm/pace that we can anticipate. When noticed we can either attack between rhythmic beats or break our own rhythm to cause a stutter in his rhythm. That can create an opening, but this must be anticipated so we can "pull the trigger" to not waste that setup.

Broken Rhythm
This refers to an unsteady pace with an uneven and unpredictable cadence within a rhythmic cycle. The three types of *Broken Rhythm*, as I teach them, are ¼ beat, ½ beat, and ¾ beat timing breaks.

The ¼ beat rhythm break refers to a quick fake or distraction. This can be a shoulder fake, hand twitch, foot stomp, knee twitch, etc., that is followed by either a same side or opposite side attack.

The ½ beat rhythm involves reaching out about halfway with a hand while reading an opponent's reaction. The weapon is then adjusted to attack in an open space created by his reaction.

The ¾ beat rhythm break refers to reaching out aggressively to touch an opponent's defense (usually his lead hand) causing his muscle structure to engage, which will then naturally briefly relax. This relaxation after engagement is when the attack is then pushed through or around his defense to attack the original target.

Tempo Changes
This refers to changing the speed or cadence of movement flow. Moving at the same speed through a motion or series of motions is okay when doing *Movement Timing,* but with *Application Timing* moving slower, faster, or alternating between them based upon an opponent's reaction is important so adjustments can be made to apply the move accurately into created openings.

This is a brief explanation of rhythm, broken rhythm, and tempo which is covered more extensively in the *Sport Fighting* chapter in the *Body*.

DIMENSIONS & ZONES

Dimensions and Zones involve having an intellectual and conceptual understanding of something that can be demonstrated physically. Like many *Concepts*, these do not need to be accepted or agreed upon to exist or be utilized as this awareness can provide a mental advantage, that can then become a physical one.

An analysis like this can help develop practical awareness of how to affect and control another person's body. A martial arts junkie can get fascinated with the intellectual evaluation of these concepts but it all simplifies when someone is trying to punch you in the face; or perhaps as his punch moves past your first two depth zones towards your upper height zone to smash your middle width zone.

An intellectual understanding of these concepts is beneficial, but my caution is to not just know this in your head/mind. Practice techniques on a live body to experience what you understand. With that said we can get under the hood and intellectualize about these important spatial concepts.

Dimensions are the three physical ways of measuring mass in the physical world. Things are measured by *height, width,* and *depth* (or length as taught in a math class). In martial arts this is taken to another level because of the interactive nature of the objects, allowing these dimensions to be broken down into dimensional space sections that then become dynamic zones. In Kenpo these are also known as *Zones of Protection, aka Zones of Attack & Defense*.

Combined, Zone concepts can further help evaluate a combatant's perspective by using the *Quadrant Zone Concept* and *6 Gates Theory*. Other zone concepts include understanding blind spots for offense and defense known as *Obscure Zones* or seeing safe areas within a chaotic and dangerous environment referred to as *Zones of Sanctuary*.

Analysis of these concepts and zones within the three-dimensional space of interacting and intersecting bodies can be used to anticipate an attacker's movement, analyze target and weapon options, provide defensive and offensive checking, manipulate, control, and to setup body positioning.

For conceptual analysis, the three individual dimensions are analyzed and referenced separately, but there is great overlap among and between them. They can be used individually, in combination, sequentially, and collectively when evaluating various techniques and positions.

Taking the *Dimensions*, and their divisions, then labeling *Zones* within those can help give us insight into the human reference perspective as it relates to a physical interaction like fighting.

These *Zones* are analyzed here on an upright person, although much of the concept transfers to the prone positions of grappling. The *Width* and *Depth Zones* both use vertical line markers, closely relating and even possibly overlapping. In contrast, the *Height Zone* uses horizontal line markers. All zones can open larger, become narrower, or even invert depending on posture.

For visual analysis, the *Height* and *Width Zones* are seen from the front of the body where the *Depth Zone* is seen from the side but once understood, the imagination can and should see them from all viewpoints. Also notice not only the zone between the lines but the lines themselves as they are in some cases more important. They are broken down as follows:

Height Zones
These are the top to bottom, head to toe, vertical measurements with horizontal dividing lines through the body, mostly where the body bends and folds around joints and body creases. The body drops and lifts through these zones.

Mr. Parker divided this into three zones from the top of the head to the solar plexus, solar plexus to bottom of groin, then groin to ground. This three-zone concept is useful for a full body analysis like how a lower body takedown fake can set up an overhand punch, or defensively how the entire body can be checked simultaneously at the upper zone shoulders, middle zone hips, and lower zone knees.

My explanation is inclusive of Mr. Parker's but viewed differently by labeling ten different *Height Zones*. This provides a smaller view of the body's sections for a more refined visual focus regarding target, weapon, and body manipulation awareness.

Many of these *Height Zones* (along with *Width* and *Depth Zones*) are based upon anatomical landmarks and the movement potential of the body's skeletal and muscular structure. It is also more closely related to the "cun" proportional body measurement system used in Traditional Chinese Medicine (TCM).

The primary difference is in accounting separately for the adaptable arms and legs. The arms are used primarily within the upper head & torso *Height Zones* and the legs mostly at, or below, the lower torso *Height Zones*. These unique and flexible body parts are also part of the *Width* and *Depth Zone* analysis.

Numbered sequentially for easier comprehension the ten *Height Zones* are divided into four *Head & Torso Zones,* three *Leg Zones,* and three *Arm Zones.*

<u>The 4 *Head/Torso Height Zones* within 5 *Horizontal Lines* are:</u>
Zone 1 – Top of head to bottom of neck (top of shoulders). This is the hinge that allows the head to move front and back, side-to-side (ear to ear), or turn left to right.

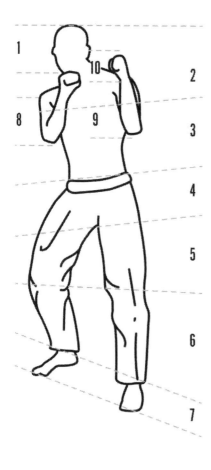

Zone 2 – Top of shoulders (bottom of neck) to bottoms of armpits (nipple line). This small but important zone is where large upper body movements start as the upper torso moves visibly from here to utilize the hands and arms strength and power.

Zone 3 – Bottom of armpits (nipple line) to waist (top of hips). Upper torso mass is moved through this zone where the body bends front and back, leans side-to-side, twists left and right, or rotates in a circle.

Zone 4 – The waist (top of hips) to the bottom of the groin. This is the location of the body center where balance and power are located. It is also where the legs are attached making it the root of their entire range of motion.

<u>The 3 *Leg Height Zones* in 4 *Horizontal Lines*</u>:
Zone 5 – Bottom of the groin (top of legs - greater trochanter) to middle patella/knee crease. This section is strongest when moving front or rear, but is also able to open (abduct), close (adduct), or circle inside and out. It moves first in most leg motions, whether to step or kick.

Zone 6 – Middle of patella (knee crease) to the ankle joints (tops of feet). This is what hinges to complete a lower leg extension or contraction. It is what reaches out when stepping or kicking where it is also able to add acceleration at the end of an upper leg movement.

Zone 7 – Ankle joints (tops of feet) to the bottoms of the feet. When standing, this is the platform needed for balance, weight transfer, and using the ground for leverage to push or spring initiating accelerated movement.

<u>The 3 *Arm Height Zones* within 4 *Horizontal Lines* are:</u>
Zone 8 – Top of shoulders to elbow joint crease that when hanging down is level with the waist. This flexible upper arm structure can be used through any direction, path, or angles of motion by swinging front and back or rotating at the shoulder. It moves the elbow and lower arm to various degrees, from straight to completely bent.

Zone 9 – Elbow joint crease to the wrist joint crease. This lower arm zone can block to protect more vulnerable areas or extend from the elbow to increase the range and acceleration of a push, strike, press, or grab. Its twisting capability also allows the hand to flexibly rotate adding acceleration while adaptively aligning with targets.

Zone 10 – Wrist joint crease to the end of the hand (fingers and knuckles). The human hand is arguably our greatest mechanical gift. In martial arts, it has the potential to be used as a blunt force instrument or a tactile tool for gripping and manipulation. Together with the wrist's capacity to flex and bend it is an extremely valuable anatomical piece.

Defensively, these *Height Zones* can be affected by pulling-down, lifting-up, pressing, through body manipulation or adjusting our body position to minimize power angles and protect vulnerable targets. Pressing or angling with these height zones in mind can eliminate the potential for an intentional counter or an unintentional reaction.

Offensive technique opportunities can be observed or created by attacking any of these zones individually, sequentially, or simultaneously. Recognizing, causing, and connecting breaks or disruptions in an opponent's height zones can affect their posture and balance making them easier to control and more vulnerable to attack.

Example: After maneuvering outside a punch (Flashing Fist) tweaking his elbow *(Zones 8/9)* then moving through to strike his kidney/ribs *(Zone 3)* causing his body to lean, where the arm is then pulled down *(Zones 8/9)*, lowering the upper torso *(Zones 1/2/3)* followed by an upward strike that lifts his head and torso *(Zones 1/2/3)*, then a downward strike onto the upper sternum *(Zone 2)*, followed up by an inward strike to his middle spine *(Zone 3)*, then a leg sweep *(Zones 4/5/6)* with another downward chest strike *(Zone 3)* driving him to the ground followed by a sweeping stomp through the feet *(Zone 7)* while exiting.

Width Zones
These are the lateral side-to-side or left and right measurements using vertical line markers through the body. It is the zone changed by torso rotation, foot pivots, and leaning sideways; and from where the limbs travel through inward and outward paths of motion.

Mr. Parker divided this into four total zones with five vertical lines where I expand that to use six zones with seven vertical lines, five inside and two outside the body. His original *Width Zones* are from the outside shoulder to middle of the breast; middle of the breast to sternum; sternum to the opposite middle breast; and that breast middle to the opposite shoulder.

This concept continues to be useful but due to the flexible nature of arm movement separate from leg movement I have split each of Mr. Parkers outside zones into two additional sections with vertical lines at the inside of the shoulders. I also prefer to visualize these lines from the centerline of the body moving outward to each side, bilaterally.

The 6 *Width Zones* within 7 *Vertical Lines* are:
Line 1 – Middle body centerline up and down along the sternum to navel line in front and the spine in back. It includes the highest point at the top of the head (GV20) to the lowest torso point at the pelvic floor (CV1). All *Width Zones* are rooted in this vertical centerline.

This is the rotational axis for torso pivoting, so when one side moves forward the other side moves behind (i.e., *Force Couple*). This makes connecting, checking, or observing an opponent's centerline a way to get advanced warning of torso movement.

Striking anywhere along this front or back centerline can be effective due to the numerous vulnerable targets contained (See *Pressure Points* in the *Body*).

Lines 2 & 3 = Zones between *Lines 1/2 & 1/3* – From the body centerline moving outwards bilaterally to each nipple. Vertical dividing lines run up the front through the collarbones in front and medial scapula in back and would include either side of the head. Moving down would include the medial hipbone in front and sacroiliac joint in the rear, along with the inside (medial) half of the legs and feet.

Checking and striking targets along this line can be used to affect posture, balance, and cause injury. Included are sides of the head and neck; medial collarbone and scapula; heart, Lv14 under the nipples; inguinal groove in the groin area; along with the inner thighs, knees, and ankles.

Lines 4 & 5 = Zones between *Lines 2/4 & 3/5* – Moves from the breast line out bilaterally to each armpit with vertical dividing lines up thru the inside angle of the shoulder and AC joint (where scapula meets collarbone) and down along the outer side of the hips, outer half of the legs and feet.

Controlling and striking along this line or inside this zone can be used to affect posture, monitor torso movement behind arm extension, and control lateral hip and leg movement. Targets include the shoulder joint, liver and spleen organs, floating ribs, outer thighs, and knees.

Lines 6 & 7 = Zones between *Lines 4/6 & 5/7* – Moving from each armpit outwards bilaterally to the outside of each shoulder, with vertical dividing lines at the furthest point outside each shoulder. Since the arms have an extensive range of motion outside of the torso and leg movement, this *Width Zone* has a tremendous capacity to change and vastly increase.

Checking along the arms or grabbing the hands, wrists, elbows, or shoulders can be used to affect arm effort while giving advanced warning of arm movement. They are attacked primarily at or near joints using the arms and hands and are also our most flexible and adaptable tool or weapon.

These six width zones, three on each side of the sternum, are at their widest when the body is squared as in a horse stance or when changing from one fighting stance to another (i.e., switching).

These zones get progressively narrower as the body is turned sideways until there are only two vertical lines outside the bodyline, leaving only one width zone when completely sideways. This means that as the width zone narrows the depth zone deepens which illustrates some of the overlap that exists between and within zones.

Having one shoulder pulled from behind (Hidden Hand) using borrowed force to step back and turn along our centerline *(Line 1)* until our arm *(Zones 5/7 & 4/6)* can strike his neck *(Line 1/2 or 1/3)* then kick *(our Zone 3/5 or 2/4)* his groin *(his Line 1)*. To complete this technique extension his inner knee *(Zones 1/2 or 1/3)* is kicked then outer collarbones *(Zones 3/5 or 2/4)* struck, followed by manipulating his torso from behind to affect his entire or all Width Zones simultaneously.

Depth Zones
These are the front to back measurements using vertical line markers through the body, most easily seen and shown here from the side, where the body can move forwards and backwards. It is also the dimension that linear projectiles travel through.

Mr. Parker saw this using eight vertical lines with his original *Depth Zones* described from a both hands up fighting stance: 1) lead hand to lead foot; 2) lead foot to lead elbow; 3) lead elbow to rear hand; 4) rear hand to face (all front side zones); 5) face to rear elbow; 6) rear elbow to rear shoulder; 7) rear shoulder to rear foot (all rear side zones).

In a static fighting posture, this progression is a useful way to look at depth zones. However, with a dynamically and unpredictable moving body this breakdown becomes clouded. My description uses joint and body landmarks that are the same regardless of posture or position. They include five depth zones with six vertical dividing lines.

The six vertical dividing lines are the emphasis in this zone concept, with the space between the lines considered the actual zones. These lines are based upon where mechanical movement begins and how it relates to attack and defense. It also accommodates the fluid nature, overlapping possibilities, and quickly changing distances that occur with interactive martial art movement.

When looking at depth or range zones the lines dramatically affect the zones they are attached to and are more easily visualized by body part. This makes them easy to comprehend and practical to recognize, control, and penetrate, even in a dynamic environment.

The 6 *Vertical Lines* enclosing the 5 *Depth Zones* are:

Line 1 / Begins Zone 1 – The most forward point or part of the body, regardless of posture, whether standing naturally, in a sport fighting stance, or the hidden fighting postures used for self-defense. Mostly the front hand and front foot but it is the literal definition of where a person's depth starts and is the first outside line.

This is the most fluid zone as the hands move flexibly and easily to attack, set up to attack, check, or defend. Attaching to or even touching this closest part of *Zone 1* can be used as an entry technique or to help check and/or damage an attacking weapon (i.e., de-fang the snake in knife fighting jargon). Offensively this is the closest to a target your most forward weapon can be.

Line 2 / Begins Zone 2 – Once engaged with another person the posture would reflect some version of a fighting stance. The next most forward body part with movement potential after the hand would be the lead elbow and/or lead knee and possibly the rear hand if near to the lead elbow. The lead elbow and knee are where limb extension is generated for striking, grabbing, or to create distance.

Checking this *depth zone* at the elbow or knee can control this hand or leg movement while providing awareness of the whole body moving. Balance can be more easily felt and manipulated by attaching to the elbow and is offensively the next closest weapon.

Line 3 / Begins Zone 3 – The next most forward joint is the lead shoulder and/or lead hip from all angles. This is where body mass is put behind the limbs for striking. Feeling and manipulating posture and especially body rotation can be checked here.

Line 4 / Begins Zone 4 – This vertical centerline of the body includes the head and groin. The depth and width zones overlap along this line as the front depth zones can quickly become the rear zones around this axis line.

This middle bodyline is where the center of balance is most easily felt and manipulated. It contains many vulnerable targets, with the head as the most prominent. Attacking lower sections of this line can affect the Height Zone as a kick to the groin can cause the upper body to move closer, with a punch to the chin possibly making it move away.

Line 5 / Begins Zone 5 - The next line is on the back or rear side of the body at the rear shoulder, hip, or knee. This is where the greatest forward power can be generated as the rear limbs can be launched and accelerated with great body mass, inertia, and momentum from this zone.

Line 6 / Ends Zone 5 – This last line is the furthest rear point of the body and is usually the lower leg or rear foot on the ground. It is where the body attaches to the ground to launch forward explosively, moving the entire body to close distance for striking or grappling. This zone is best checked through a preemptive attack, by angling away, or moving behind the opponent's lead foot.

In response to a step-thru punch (Compulsive Kneel), the punching hand is caught with one hand *(Line 1)*, then the elbow checked with the other hand *(Line 2)*, before sliding to grab the lead shoulder *(Line 3)*, before then stepping behind to grab their opposite shoulder *(Line 5)* to pull them back off balance *(Line 4)* before kicking their far leg to buckle their knee and foot to the ground *(Line 6)*.

Summary: *Height, Width,* and *Depth Dimensional Zones* are usually in flux, so they may be larger, smaller, overlap, or be nonexistent depending on someone's body position and posture at any given moment. If squatting down with the hands on the ground most *Vertical Zones* disappear; if turned sideways most of the *Width Zones* do the same, if standing square *Depth Zones* overlap.

Practicing with these zones in mind can however help give a better understanding of where we can be effective or where an opponent is dangerous, or vulnerable. They are a good evaluative tool to help see where to attack, how to attack, how to create an opening, and what will happen when a body is in motion or manipulated in a certain direction, plus how to check and minimize our own openings.

Quadrant Zone Theory
Mr. Parker used this to divide the body into 4 three-dimensional zones, or gates, that overlap with his *Outer Rim Theory*. Using the centerline as a vertical marker (sagittal plane) and the solar plexus as a horizontal marker (transverse plane), the torso is divided into upper right, upper left, lower right, and lower left zones (coronal plane).

This concept works especially well for upper body analysis. It is also part of the formulation matrix for the Kenpo knife defense system (see "Knife Defense Formula" video).

Gate Theory
This is a commonly used concept in Chinese martial arts that sees 6 gates that contain the same 3 *Height Zones* used by Mr. Parker but with a centerline, like in his *Quadrant Zone Concept*, but includes the legs for a more thorough grappling, leg attack, and balance disruption analysis.

6 Gates: *Upper Right & Left, Middle Right & Left,* and *Lower Right & Left.* These are not accessible or open from every position.

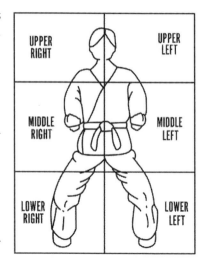

The upper 4 quadrants are where the arms are primarily utilized with the upper body able to move in different directions to set up and avoid attack. For example, to avoid punches a boxer will lean (slip) into his upper right or left quadrants. He may also bend his legs to move down then up while moving side to side to avoid punches (bob & weave).

If a fighter drops levels merging from 4 gates to 2, as often done in wrestling, then better grappling leverage is attained. If only one fighter were to change levels for grappling while the other fighter was still upright, then the wrestler would have a grappling advantage with the upright fighter a footwork and striking advantage, provided he can defend his legs from being grabbed.

Whatever the conceptual preference dividing the body into *4 Zones* or *6 Gates* makes for smaller areas of analysis of attack or defense, un-complicating the possibilities.

Obscure Zones
These are angles or blind spots that we, or an opponent, cannot see from the inside looking out through our own eyes. Also known in Kenpo as *Zones of Obscurity* they include under the chin, under the groin, top of the head, plus any backside body or head target. Basically, it's any part of ourselves that we cannot see without a mirror.

These blind spots are protected defensively through checking and angling and can be attacked offensively with effective results since an opponent cannot see an attack moving into a blind spot area.

Anyone who has played contact sports knows that the hit you don't see coming is the one that hurts the most and can be the most devastating as the mind and body are not prepared for the contact. This concept takes advantage of that reality.

Zone(s) of Sanctuary
These refer to safe places within a chaotic situation or a dynamic and dangerous position that provide a place to avoid injury, regroup, and ride-out an attack until something changes.

This is an expanded explanation of Ed Parkers original definition as "dead areas of space where you can position yourself for protection." Although his definition is good there is a tendency to limit this to only moving outside of a dangerous path.

The classic teaching example in Kenpo puts a circle inside of a square leaving 4 open corners outside of the circle (Returning Club). This example describes swinging a club but could also apply to a fist or leg attack by placing our initial defense outside the circumference of the circular motion attack. This describes an "outside" zone of sanctuary.

In my analysis these zones are divided into not only "outside" but "inside" safe zones as well. That same club attack has an *inside* zone found by moving to the base of the weapon (i.e., the eye of the storm) thereby cancelling the range benefit of that weapon.

Another of these *Sanctuary Zones* is at the rear corner of an opponent's shoulder. An attacker shaking our hand could still punch with their free hand but moving outside their arm and/or behind their shoulder neutralizes that punch (Destructive Gift).

These zones are also used in grappling. Ducking a striker's jab and placing the back of our head behind his shoulder then pressing back can help us to move behind him. Once behind then our head can press against his upper back to minimize the effect of backward strikes, before possibly moving to a takedown.

An *inside Zone of Sanctuary* also mirrors the concept of riding the storm and is analogous to going to the "eye of the storm" as described earlier. This refers to maintaining a safe position until the storm passes, dissipates, or where we can work to escape.

Defending a submission attempt where, although still grasped, the effective ability of the attack is neutralized. These different scenarios can and should be practiced, i.e. *bad position drills*, where we must find safe zones to survive within until an escape can be made. This is done by causing discomfort to the attacker and then transitioning to a better position until eventually out of danger.

Summary: *Dimensions and Zones* are useful visuals for our minds to comprehend and pre-determine an opponent's positioning for attack or defense. Analysis of these zones can be used to determine weapon/target possibilities, and an opponent's intention along with defensive and offensive checking. Again, know these physically and not just in your mind.

CONTOURING

Contouring refers to using our body shape and dimensions, or that of an opponent, as a guide to help with the alignment of an intended martial art movement. Ed Parker divided these into *Body Contact* and *Non-Body Contact* methods. Since all methods are designed to apply body contact they are split here into *Contouring Methods for Striking* and *Contouring Methods for Checking*. Even though strikes can check, and checks can strike, the applied intention is what makes them different.

Ed Parker coined the idea of *Contouring* using terms such as: *Launching, Leveraging, Sliding Check, Frictional Pull, Tracking, Guidelining, Threading, Needling, Pivoting, Windshield Wiper, Fitting, Gravitational Checks, Pressing Checks, Complimentary Angle, Framing, Angle Matching, Silhouetting,* along with *Symmetrical* and *Corresponding Angles.*

These are scattered throughout his works, making them seem difficult to grasp as one concept, so I have tried to tie them together into one cohesive explanation. There is a fair amount of overlap and some redundancy among many of those original terms, so I have attempted to clarify them.

For example, *Guidelining* is a *Complimentary Angle* with contact, *Windshield Wiper* uses *Pivoting*, and *Angle Matching* fits several terms including *Silhouetting*. *Complimentary Angle* and *Sliding* are also similar, as is *Framing* and the *Geometric Symbol Concept*, along with *Gravitational Checks* and *Pressing Checks*, *Rebounding* and *Launching*, with some just poorly named, like *Needling*.

To make this subject more understandable and easier to use I have combined, dropped, and renamed some terms while explaining some obvious overlaps. Mr. Parker's terms are italicized for reference, should the reader prefer those original terms.

Contouring Methods for Striking:
Fitting is the only *body contact method* that Mr. Parker discussed in the *Contouring* discussion of his Book 4. It is when a weapon is used that is shaped to fit a specific target, i.e. *Puzzle Principle*, like how the bent elbow tip fits nicely into the solar plexus (Hidden Elbow) or a hammerfist fits into the pocket at the side of the nose (Fist of Aggression).

Launching uses one surface to bounce/rebound, lever, or push off towards another targeted surface. This can be from the ground with the feet accelerating the entire body forward (Snapping Arm) or is used to provide leverage when changing stances (Darting Fist) or rebounding off our own body (Six Hands) or an opponent's (Glancing Palm). Even bouncing the lead hand off our own thigh, as seen in sport fighting, uses this idea to gain hand acceleration.

Tracking is a line of action where a limb moves close to our own limb (Circling the Arm), or slides along an opponent's limbs (Six Hands), or wedges through a small space (Blinding Vice). This can also be done before body contact is made as the other definition of tracking has to do with moving along a precise path.

Complimentary Angle follows a path or angle that parallels a part of an opponent's body and is the only *non-body contact method* Mr. Parker mentions in his Book 4 *Contouring* discussion. It is used here like tracking but is more a path of action than a line of action.

This is when an entire surface area is used to guide a weapon to a target like an obscure elbow strike (Captured Arms) or a forearm under the chin (Sweeping the Leg). Other related Ed Parker terms that can fit under this heading are *Framing, Angle Matching, Silhouetting, Symmetrical* and *Corresponding Angles*.

Contouring Methods of Checking:
Feel refers to the feet or hands as they slide from one place to another while staying lightly connected. The hands and arms can move as a *sliding check*, pivot on a surface like a *windshield wiper,* or drag along a body part causing *frictional pull*. These are done to check, affect balance, transition to another position, act as a location reference, or possibly cause damage.

Examples include sliding the forearm down along an opponent's forearms using frictional pull (Twin Lapel Grab), pivoting on the jaw scraping the fingers back and forth across the eyes (Turning Windmills), or pivoting an upward palm strike around an elbow to clear that arm (Snapping Arm).

Leveraging is when part of an opponent's body is used as a *fulcrum* or *pivot point* with a *bracing angle* causing them to be controlled or injured. This is done to cancel (Hammerlock), align a target (Escaping Death), or accelerate their body into another attack (Triggered Palm). See *'Mechanical Advantage'* section in this books Physical Principles chapter.

Pressing is a force used after attaching on or along an opponent's body as a location reference (Entangled Arm B), to change their posture or position (The Nutcracker), for checking (Buckling the Leg), or to attack sensitive areas causing pain and injury (Grabbing Hair).

Contouring Summary
This useful visual looks at an opponent's body like a puzzle and our weapons as pieces that fit onto or into the different puzzle openings. Using the best weapon to fit a target at the most effective angle and at the right time is what makes them correct. This optimum and effective utilization is the essence of good martial arts technique as studied, analyzed, understood, and practiced.

TARGETS

Whether giving or receiving, a target must be accessible to become vulnerable to an effective attack. Hopefully, we are giving more than receiving but a colleague and friend Sharkey LeCroy (Kenpo Black Belt and former Texas State Kickboxing Champion) said it this way. "We are friendly when fighting because we don't hit them where they don't want us too. If their hands are up that means they don't want to get hit there, so we hit them low, where they want to get hit; if they protect low, we hit high because it is the friendly thing to do."

Kidding aside, the point is to not chase unavailable targets just to use your favorite move. Attacking the most accessible target may however require you to have more tools, i.e. weapons and methods.

Developing fighting skills at different ranges and angles, learning how to strike, press, and hold the body in every viable way increases the number of options available in fighting technique. Learning effective and logical combinations that analyze or create openings from various angles, or which weapon(s) work best against those openings are all factors in recognizing, creating, and utilizing target vulnerability.

Methods to open targets include a low kick to bend the torso forward (Thrusting Palm), or a manipulation that pulls them down (Six Hands), tilting the head sideways to compress the neck (Raking Fist), lifting the chin to stretch and expose the throat (Pursuing Panther), lifting the chin to open the torso to striking (Sweeping the Leg), striking the neck to bring the head forward into another strike (Snapping Arm), poking the eyes to lift the hands and stretch the torso (Blinding Vice), etc.

Also important are the shape of a weapon, how they *contour* to fit the shape of a target surface, and how the body and limbs align to follow the best entry angle, then how it makes contact at the most effective vector.

Keep in mind what contact athletes already know, "it hurts more if you don't see it coming." Keep natural *obscure zones*, i.e. blind spots, in mind when choosing targets or create them with setup techniques that manipulate, cause a reflex, distract and/or block vision, and always protect your own *obscure zones*.

Target knowledge is best developed and practiced with live training partners using controlled but effective technique. This can be practiced while doing prearranged attack/defense patterns, spontaneous street attack scenarios, or sparring. These are important to provide the reps and variations needed to develop the visual awareness, mental recognition, muscle memory, timing, and experience needed for success.

WEAPONS

We have all heard the expression, "use the right tool for the job." This applies to weapon/target selection as well. Do not punch someone's skull, do not finger jab his sternum, do not kick someone a foot taller than you in the head and do not head butt his foot. Get the idea?

If you must strike someone's skull, without hand gear, use a palm strike or a hammerfist. If you cannot resist punching the head try punching the temple, jaw hinge, across or under the chin, nose, or eye socket. If you get the urge to finger strike the chest try a middle knuckle punch. Kick that tall guy in the groin or knee and when he bends over then kick him in the head, and in any case never head butt someone's foot.

Punching the head is popular in sport fighting but in the street, without protective equipment, the skull is low on the list of targets for the knuckles to punch, although I get that sometimes you just want to punch someone in the face. Just remember that the small punching knuckles as easily broken on someone's hard skull and the wrist alignment when punching can be difficult to maintain with heavy contact.

This is compounded by the fact that targets move unpredictably in a fight so what was an opening to the ribs suddenly moves closer and/or is blocked by the more durable elbow before your knuckle gets there it's easy to jam the wrist and hand which can cause damage.

Since opponents are going to make it as difficult as possible for you to hit them, it means targets will be changing angles and distance constantly. This makes it difficult to hit exactly where intended and with leverage. This is where setups and *Point of Origin* attacks are important for alignment in attacking targets that are open and not prepared for contact.

Boxers are experts at punching but the first thing a boxer does before entering the ring is to wrap his hands and wrists. This is because they know the dangers of punching with the unsupported and unreinforced bones that make up the hand.

There are often many choices when selecting the right weapon for the target, or tool for the job. Evaluate and practice this in training by determining the best weapons available and how they match available targets. Many times it is punching but often another tool will do the job at least as well and with less risk of injury to our self.

This takes analyzing the skills that work in different situations and, just like with a fire drill, waiting for the fire to break out is not the time to figure out where the extinguishers are and how to get out of the building.

EQUATION FORMULA

This was developed by the late Kenpo Grand Master Edmund K Parker and is listed in Book 5 of his "Infinite Insights" series. It is a brilliant concept that I have expanded upon slightly to include a few things which I felt were not fully covered in the original. Grafting is another related concept discussed in this section.

The Kenpo self-defense technique called Delayed Hand (EPAK Delayed Sword) will be used to explain the *Equation Formula* and each of its eight variables. In this technique an attacker is either grabbing the lapel with his right hand or throwing a high right punch that we can get inside of.

Base Technique: 1) Step back left into a right neutral bow with a right inward block inside attacker's right wrist, with a left-hand position check nearby. 2) Right front snap-kick his groin. 3) Settle your weight with a right outward handsword strike to the right side of his neck, and then quickly return that hand to the previous blocking position.

The *Equation Formula* was designed to help analyze and reformulate the prearranged self-defense technique combinations in the Kenpo system. This allows for unlimited flexibility and adaptation to the lessons contained while addressing any "what ifs" that could come up. The premise of the formula is that for any given technique the following changes can be made individually or in combination: Prefix – Suffix – Insert – Delete – Rearrange – Alter – Regulate – Adjust.

PREFIX
ADD a move before the initial move in a technique, including pre-emptive striking. Examples: Putting a left outward parry before the right inward block (move #1), or perhaps the opponent is close enough to rake his nose with a right inward hammerfist on the path to blocking his arm.

SUFFIX
ADD a move to the end of a technique. Examples: After move #3's outward handsword strike, possibilities include a right front scoop kick through his groin to exit or a left step thru front push kick to clear him away; and possibly repeatedly adding moves on until the fight is won.

INSERT
ADD a move somewhere between the other moves. Examples: After the initial block (move #1) and before the right front snap kick (move #2) insert a left inverted side kick (TSK) to his front knee, or after the right front snap kick (move #2) but before the right outward handsword strike (move #3) do right side stomp on his foot or a right outward elbow strike to his temple.

DELETE
Take a move out of the technique. Examples: Blocking (1) followed by chopping the neck (3) leaving the kick out or blocking (1) then only kicking (2), or a pre-emptive kick (2) with no block before the handsword (3).

REARRANGE
Change two or more moves within the sequence of a base technique. Examples: A three move technique, such as Delayed Hand/Sword, could theoretically have six different sequences: The original block-kick-strike; block-strike-kick; kick-strike-block; kick-block-strike; strike-block-kick; strike-kick-block.

ALTER
Change the weapon and/or target in a technique sequence. Examples: After the initial block instead of kicking his groin adjust to kick his knee or solar plexus, or if closer a right knee followed by an outward elbow, etc.

REGULATE
Change the tempo, timing, or emphasis of moves within a technique sequence. Examples: The block and kick could be done more quickly in preparation for major emphasis on the handsword strike, or the groin kick could have more emphasis followed by a quicker snapping neck strike, etc.

ADJUST
Change the height, width, depth, (i.e. body position) in a technique sequence using these individually, collectively, or in combination by maneuvering the feet, legs, or torso to align the body for better defensive or offensive positioning.

Height Example: A height adjustment drops lower or lifts under an opponent so ducking under his right punch before front kicking his groin then chopping his neck. This helps if attacked by a much shorter or taller person where we could drop our stance to align with lower targets or stay taller for better vision.

Width Example: A width adjustment changes the angle relative to the opponent. Stepping back left but slightly off angle to a 4:30-10:30 line to obtain a stronger alignment into the attacker's weaker line, or perhaps an upper body slip motion before finishing with the kick and handsword strike.

Depth Example: A depth adjustment changes the distance between us and the opponent. If the attacker lunges forward with his punch then stepping back further can help avoid his effort or perhaps our front kick drives him back making it necessary to shuffle forward after to help us reach him with the handsword strike.

Adjust can also refer to what happens if we force an opponent to change their position by striking, checking, pushing, pulling, or canceling them. If the groin kick makes them collapse to the ground or causes them to turn completely sideways while bending over then we would have to adapt and adjust to this unanticipated position.

GRAFTING is a related idea in that it can take place within or after a technique sequence. It involves the blending or borrowing of movements from more than one pre-arranged technique sequence based upon changing circumstances and then linking, connecting, or *grafting* them together. These essentially limitless arrangements relate to the idea of *Master Keys* in various basics, movements, and organized techniques.

Punch Attack Example:
After applying a lead hand inward block, then expecting to front kick the groin (Delayed Hand), the opponent throws an opposite hand round punch causing us to do an extended outward block inside that second punch, as we either simultaneously punch them in the face with our opposite hand (Fatal Variation) or then front kick their groin (Hand of Destruction) or switch to a rear hand inward block (Pursuing Panther). Each would have their own follow-ups unless more grafting was needed.

Rear Bear Hug Attack Example:
Defending a bear hug from behind involves tenderizing techniques and shifting the hips to avoid being lifted. If between their feet we could do a foot stomp followed by an obscure elbow strike under his chin (Captured Arms) or a rear sliding leg sweep through his knee (Sweeping the Leg) or a knee buckle (Scraping Stomp) or spin out trapping his elbow (Spiraling Wrist).

If in the Rear Bear Hug example our feet are positioned more to the side, where one of their feet can be seen between ours, then we could step around their leg to get our hip behind theirs where grappling (Crushing Palm) or striking (Crashing Elbows) can be done, or if not able to get behind them then we could reach down and pick up their leg between our legs (Straddling the Leg).

Push to a Grab Example:
Stepping back against a low push/grab attempt while separating their arms then groin kicking them followed by an inward hammerfist (Hooking Arms) but if the hammerfist were blocked we could then drive a forward vertical elbow strike into their chest grafting into a new technique sequence (Entangled Arm B).

Etc...

LEVELS OF FORCE

The degrees of physical damage inflicted upon another person. The 7 *Levels of Force* listed here can occur intentionally or unintentionally or be a combination of what was meant to happen and what actually happened.

Humans also have moral considerations when trying to harm another person so the intention behind any level of force can only be determined by the mind and each person's moral code, with them ultimately responsible for that decision. Intentionally causing permanent disability or death would only be justified in rare situations, or in war.

The 7 Levels of Force are:

Level #1: Distraction / Attention Getter – Any technique or application that gets another person to focus or refocus their mind and/or their eyes.

Level #2: Control & Discomfort – Any technique or application that neutralizes an opponent's efforts by holding them in place, forcing compliance, or causing discomfort in a way that cancels their attempts to cause harm.

Level #3: Strain & Sprain – Any technique or application that temporarily damages any part of an opponent's anatomy (internal or external) causing a level of pain and dysfunction that ends their attempts to cause harm at that moment.

Level #4: Break & Dislocate – Any technique or application that stops someone's ability to cause harm due to pain and/or anatomical dysfunction by the breaking of bones or dislocation of joints.

Level #5: Unconsciousness or Knockout – Any technique or application that causes an opponent to lose his mental awareness and function for a limited time ranging from temporary dizziness, to relaxed sleep, to a rigid tonic seizure. These are generally recoverable long term but a fight ender short term.

Level #6: Disable – Any technique or application that damages an opponent in a way from which they will never fully recover. This can range from joint disfigurement, an injury affecting the spine, an internal organ, sight, or the effectiveness of the mind as in brain damage. Although permanent long term it may not be a fight ender short term.

Level #7: Death or Kill – Any technique or application that causes the death of another person. This should be avoided if humanly possible.

PHYSICAL PRINCIPLES
Chapter IV

Physical Principles are the observable part of martial arts. They are how the human body can be positioned or moved to accumulate and transfer energy and power or provide resistance through structure and alignment. Not only are these used to move our own body but, in martial arts, they are also done interactively to move and affect another body.

Combined with the "internal" (Yin) *Mental Concept* awareness covered in the previous chapter these *Physical Principles*, or "external" (Yang), training components are where applied interactive motion is used to develop, regulate, and apply our own power most efficiently and effectively. All while giving us the awareness and understanding of how to read and control another person's structural potential.

19 of these "Physical Principles" used in martial arts are listed here.

The first group, *Motion & Movement, Movement (Muscle) Preload, Muscular Acceleration, Whipping Acceleration, Springloading, Wave Transference, Torque/Rotation, Dropping/Settling, Lifting/Rising, Collapsing/Compressing, Expanding, Rebounding,* and *Stretch Reflex Acceleration* occur within an individual structure, with the option to be applied onto another structure.

The second group, *Major/Minor Principle and Mechanical Advantage* occur within our own structure but are applied relative to another structure.

The third group, *Borrowed Force, Voluntary Momentum, Manipulated Voluntary Momentum,* and *Involuntary Momentum* use another structure against itself.

Isolating and understanding these *Physical Principles* individually is a useful way to comprehend them but know that they are utilized holistically. Some have multiple aspects but together, when combined *simultaneously* or connected *sequentially,* they can be compounded in limitless ways.

Simultaneously, a closed fist is applied using *Muscular Acceleration* via *Wave Transference* while applying *Mechanical Advantage* and is almost always accompanied by *Torque* with footwork able to add *Voluntary Momentum* that may generate some *Involuntary Momentum.*

Sequentially, a *Lifting/Rising* motion is often followed by a *Dropping/Settling* motion which pre-loads the legs for an explosive *Expanding* action that can then be followed by a *Collapsing* action.

Kenpo techniques in parenthesis illustrating one of these Physical Principles can be seen at BarryBBarker.com

MOTION & MOVEMENT

Martial arts are a movement and applied motion science with the universal truth that all things, and especially people, are always in motion to some degree or another.

Several types of *Motion* become the content that makes for *Movement*, which is done in a context with intention to accomplish an objective. Those objectives run the gamut of human need and interest from martial arts to dance to sport, etc.

The study of motion and movement is the study of linked kinetic human activity done individually or connected interactively with another person for exercise, skill development, muscle memory, visualization training, or applied onto an inanimate object like a brick.

Setting aside the importance of *timing*, this kinetic motion can be applied using *velocity* and *acceleration* to move *mass*, creating *force*. The discussion here however relates only to human *Motion & Movement* with analysis of the *Language of Motion, Motion & Movement Organization, Motion & Movement Applications, Methods of Mechanical Motion, Alignment of Muscular Force, Characteristics of Acceleration, Point of Contact Variables, States of Matter,* and *Ed Parker's Universal Pattern*.

From simple mechanical principles to complex concepts these can produce intricate and sophisticated combinations of kinetic human movement that, with intention, becomes useful motion.

Language of Motion
This analogy relates the English language with the movements of Kenpo. It is originally attributed to the late Kenpo Grandmaster Edmund K Parker, with my concept and explanation slightly different. Here is my take.

Any single mechanical motion or intended movement is a *Letter*. Lifting your bent knee into the air would be a letter that primarily uses the hip flexors and lower abdominal muscles. When several of these individual mechanical movements are linked together, as in *Basics*, those become *Words* of motion.

Mr. Parker's analogy used *Basics* as the "alphabet of motion" where in my explanation each mechanical motion is a letter in that alphabet. It is like how the English alphabet needs 26 letters to make every word (my concept) where the Chinese language uses thousands of characters to do the same thing (Mr. Parker's concept).

A front snap kick therefore requires four mechanical movements or *letters*: Lifting the knee (hip flexor), kicking the foot forward (quadriceps), retracting the foot (hamstrings), and placing it on the ground (glutes).

Since every kick to the front or side of the body starts with lifting the knee, this motion (i.e. letter) begins most kicks. It is therefore a separate *letter* in a sequence of mechanical motions that make the front snap kick a *word*.

Everything else flows from that premise meaning combined *Basics* then make *Sentences* so stepping back against a punch attack to create space, perhaps into a fighting stance, would be a *word*. If combined with an inward block, also a *word*, and a position check, another *word*, then a *sentence* of motion would be made.

A *sentence* requires a noun or subject (e.g., the punch), a verb is an action (e.g., the block), and in the example above a couple of adverbs adding to the verb (e.g., the fighting stance and position check).

By putting several sentences together then a *Paragraph* of motion is formed to complete a thought. So then by adding a front snap kick followed by an outward handsword strike that makes the Kenpo self-defense technique called "Delayed Hand/Sword," aka a *paragraph* of motion.

Other arrangements of motion in Kenpo are called *Sets* (i.e., movement patterns). These are used to index and practice a certain type of *Basic*. This just means that Stance Sets practice stance sequences, "Kicking Sets" do this with kicking, and "Blocking Sets" with blocking, etc.

We also know from studying language that it takes *paragraphs* to make *Chapters,* and several *chapters* to tell a *Story* or write a book. Putting similar *Sets* together, like all Kicking or Stance Sets, would make a *chapter* of motion with that as the theme.

Putting a group of *Self-Defense Techniques* together within a martial theme would be the *Forms/Katas* or martial arts, or a *chapter* of motion. Kenpo has six of these empty-handed Forms (#1-6) ranging from simple to complex.

An advanced practitioner, like a language scholar, can find the complex in the simple. A defensive blocking pattern, like Kenpo Short Form 1, in the hands and mind of a master practitioner can take on a whole variety of meanings above and beyond what a beginner might see or be shown.

When several *chapters* are put together they tell a *story* of motion, which in this context is synonymous to a martial art system. There are many different systems of martial arts whose stories range in theme and depth. Kenpo is a street self-defense system with some sport fighting thrown in for fun, competition, and to gain live spontaneous fighting experience.

Kenpo *chapters* telling that martial art system story include *Basics, Sets, Forms, Sport Fighting,* and *Self-Defense techniques.* These are all explained more extensively in my book on the *Body.* Other martial arts styles have their own *story* so may have similar or different chapter headings.

Some martial arts are movement or performance based, others focus on sport fighting, or others on weapons, etc. The list of styles can seem endless, but all are rooted in the same kinetic human movement with an emphasis based upon the goals of the style and the intention of the practitioner.

Language of Motion Analogy Summary:
Alphabet – Individual mechanical kinetic movement

Example: Make a fist, bend your elbow to lift your hand, move your forearm across in front of your face. These three separate mechanical motions, i.e. *letters,* make the *Basic* or *word* that we call an Inward Block.

Words – Individual mechanical movements combined to form *Basics*.

Example: Lift your knee, extend your foot, retract your foot, put it on the ground to make up the four mechanical movements of a Front Snap Kick.

Sentences – Combining several *words* or *Basics* together simultaneously.

Example: Step back to a fighting stance with a lead hand inward block and rear hand position check or move #1 in the Self-Defense Technique called Delayed Hand/Sword.

Paragraphs – Using several *sentences* together in a sequence to make a Self-Defense Technique, a Set, or a Form.

Example: Self-Defense Technique "Delayed Hand/Sword"
Sentence #1 – Step back left to right neutral bow fighting stance with a right inward block and left-hand position check.
Sentence #2 – Transition back through a right cat stance then right front snap kick maintaining right block and left-hand position check.
Sentence #3 – Step down forward to a right neutral bow stance with a right outward handsword strike that then returns to a blocking position while the left hand remains as a position check.

Example: Stance Set 1
From a standing horse stance: step back left to a right neutral bow stance; adjust to a right forward bow stance, then right close kneel stance, right forward bow stance; and return to right neutral bow stance, then to a right cat stance; defensive switch to a left neutral bow stance; repeat previous pattern with left leg in front and then return to standing horse stance.

Chapters – Combined *paragraphs* explaining a thought.

Example: *Sets* – Putting paragraphs together by theme such as Stance Set 1 followed by Stance Set 2 followed by Stance Set 3 (see the *Body*).

Example: *Forms* – Combining minor and major themes with combined basics through a sequence. Kenpo beginner's Short and Long Form 1 index *Master Key Motions* of the arms while practicing defensive footwork and stances. Other forms cover other important themes. See *Movement Routines* chapter in the *Body*.

Stories – The human *alphabet* of movement used in the martial art context can be put into *words*, combined into *sentences*, formulated into *paragraphs*, and organized into *chapters* to make up a *System*.

How well movements are physically done, whether single basics, combined basics, technique sequences, and indexed patterns, i.e. "said," is where the rubber hits the road with this analogy.

Movement, like speech should not be monotone, as cadence and inflection are varied in both. Intellectual understanding aside, this gets into a whole discussion of enunciation, e.g. movement precision and grammatical speech, e.g. proper mechanics.

A martial art *story* can be used or demonstrated to varying levels depending on instruction, training, and talent. Slurred speech, like slurred motion, does not sound pleasant and is difficult to understand or watch in this case, although the person making the effort may still enjoy the process and may even gain some personal benefit from the practice.

A martial art done at the highest levels is like a trained and talented linguist who can captivate an audience with an impassioned soliloquy, or a slick politician who can dazzle the masses, or the street rapper who can improvise a rhyme, or the poet/songwriter who can move our spirit with insightful and passionate words.

Defined and organized *motion* and *movement* is analogous in many ways to not only the written word but also the spoken language, therefore, lessons learned in one can be correlated to lessons learned in the other. This can make for a more thorough intellectual understanding that can lead to more sophisticated prose, e.g. better execution of motion.

Motion & Movement Organization
Mr. Parker did an outstanding job of organizing, labelling, and listing basics in his *Infinite Insights into Kenpo* series Book 3 on *Physical Analyzation*. Rather than repeat what he already did so well I will defer the reader and recommend the *Organizational Chart of Motion and Movement* in that book. Covered here are the applications of those motions and the movements needed to execute them.

Motion & Movement Applications
There are multiple variables that together make for the matrix of human movement, especially the applied movement as done in martial arts. They are broken down here into the distinct components of *Directions of Motion, Paths of Motion, Angles of*

Motion, Dimensions of Motion, Methods of Mechanical Motion, Alignment of Muscular Force, Characteristics of Acceleration, and *Point of Contact Variables.*

Note: Mr. Parker's original seven "Methods of Striking" are *Thrust, Whip, Roundhouse, Hook, Slice, Hammer,* and *Claw.* Those are included here but broken down further while adding a few other important categories and applied movement definitions.

The penetrating *Thrust,* powerfully contracting *Hook,* and explosive *Whip* are listed and discussed here under *Characteristics of Acceleration,* along with the dynamic *Snap. Slice* and *Claw* are here as sub-categories that occur once contact has been made with *Roundhouse and Hammer* motions used with a few different natural weapons and applied using different characteristics, so they are listed under *Methods of Mechanical Motion.*

Although not necessarily universal, the terms presented here are appropriate and accurate for the martial art actions described. There is flexibility in the concept however as a *Whip* motion can travel through or snap back, a *Thrust* can stick, push, or return with a snap, etc.

Directions of Motion: *(The Vector of Travel between Points)*
1. Forward   *(Front)*
2. Backward   *(Rear or Behind)*
3. Sideways   *(Left to Right; Right to Left)*
4. Inward   *(Towards the Centerline)*
5. Outward   *(Away from the Centerline)*
6. Upward   *(Above)*
7. Downward   *(Below)*

Paths of Motion: *(The Trajectory of a Moving Object)*
1. Linear   *(Moving in a Straight Line)*
2. Circular   *(Following a Curved or Arced Path)*

Angles of Motion: *(The Route or Course)*
1. Horizontal   *(Side to Side)*
2. Vertical   *(Up and Down)*
3. Diagonal   *(Degrees between Horizontal & Vertical)*

Dimensions of Motion: *(3 Physical Ways of Measuring)*
1. Height   *(Top to Bottom / Bottom to Top)*
2. Width   *(Left to Right / Right to Left)*
3. Depth   *(Front to Back / Back to Front)*

Listing these *Directions, Paths, Angles,* and *Dimensions of Motion* separately can minimize the importance of how they connect and interact so don't lose that in the list. *Directions* and *Angles* whether on whole or on parts of the body change constantly where linear *Paths* connect with circular and circular connects to linear often in movement and *Dimensions* always a fluid dynamic.

Methods of Mechanical Motion

These are the *letters* in the *Language of Motion* which are the functional ranges of motion (ROM) that muscles and joints of the arms and legs can perform while applying, in this case, martial art technique.

These unique individual mechanical movements of the four limbs are used by connecting them sequentially as part of a kinetic movement chain that is applied fluidly as a *Wave Transference* of motion. They are isolated here into individual motions of the *Arm: Shoulder - Elbow - Forearm - Wrist – Hand* and *Leg: Hip - Knee - Ankle - Toes*, with examples of their use.

Defensively, the goal would be to defeat these structures by knowing how they are most effectively applied to avoid or interrupt those correct paths of motion by using various methods of disruption. This is enhanced by an understanding of the structures and functions involved.

Note: The terms used to describe the following motions and applied movements are a mixture of Western medical and sports vernacular, plus terms common to martial arts or other movement disciplines.

Arm: Shoulder - Elbow - Forearm - Wrist - Hand

Shoulder: Arm Swing – This ball and socket joint is where the upper arm (humerus bone) connects to the torso and hinges at the shoulder like a pendulum capable of a 360° circle using the 4 rotator cuff muscles (supraspinatus, infraspinatus, teres minor, and subscapularus).

Ignoring the forearm and hand for the moment, and just focusing on elbow movement, shoulder motions are swinging front/back (flexion/extension), outward away from the centerline (abduction) or inward towards the body centerline (adduction). The other shoulder motion is known as "rotation" where the elbow can move in a circle and is used when applying shoulder locks such as the Kimura, Americana, and Hammerlock.

Forearm motions working with elbow/shoulder motions, and wrist motions working with forearm motions, are often used in martial arts to accelerate, enunciate, and compound force to impact as part of *Wave Transference*.

Examples: Double inward roundhouse punch (Blinding Vice), overhead downward handsword (Charging Tackle); upward stiff-arm punch (Spiraling Wrist); forward/inward forearm (Thundering Fists), deflecting downward block (Deflecting, Hugging, and Retreating Pendulum).

Elbow: Straighten/Bend – This is where the lower arm hinges at the elbow. Straightening the forearm extends the hand (triceps) and can take several shapes (hammerfist, handsword, etc.). Bending the arm (bicep) retracts the forearm for striking (upward reverse hammerfist) or grappling (sleeper choke). These motions can also be done in conjunction with the shoulder swinging motion such as straightening the elbow into an outward whipping backknuckle or bending it into a reverse handsword/ridgehand.

Examples: An upward reverse hammerfist (Circling the Arm); sleeper choke after turning an attacker around (Turn of Fate), inward hooking backknuckle to mastoid (Twirling Fist).

Forearm: Internal Rotation (pronate) / External Rotation (supinate) – This is the lower arm turning whether initiated at the forearms or the hand(s).

Internal Rotation: Turning the hand <u>palm down</u> (pronation) initiates this forearm action which is also a component of punching forward. This wrist/forearm twisting is an important link in the kinetic striking chain using the hands and arms and is where much of the explosive acceleration takes place into a target.

Examples: Fingers-in palm strike (Tripping Leg); extended block (Shielding Fingers); upward flapping elbow strike (Twin Lapel Grab); twisting the hand into a wrist come-a-long hold (Twisting the Gift) .

External Rotation – Turning the hand <u>palm up</u> (supination) initiates this forearm action as the hand and forearm twist together, often with a lat contraction. This is another important link in the kinetic striking chain of the hands and arms.

Examples: Outward hooking check (Begging Palms); outward whipping backknuckle (Thundering Fists); inward downward hammerfist (Crashing Elbows); twisting the hand to change posture (Returning the Gift).

These methods can also be combined with internal followed by external or external followed by internal forearm rotation motions each adding acceleration and power to the other.

Examples: Extended block/inward hammerfist (Shielding Fingers); inward block/outward handsword (Six Hands); downward flapping elbow turning palm up followed by an inward elbow turning palm down (Fist of Aggression); Moves 1-2-3 in *Blocking Set*.

<u>Wrist: Extension - Flexion - Ulnar Flexion - Radial Flexion</u>
The four main directions that the wrist bends, inclusive of the combined circular rotation they allow, are important end-of-line links in the arms kinetic striking chain and where much of a weapons penetration speed into a target is generated.

Extension – Bending the wrist to move the <u>back of knuckles and open fingertips</u> towards the lateral forearm, as the medial wrist can move in the opposite direction with the application intention in either direction with various weapon options.

Examples: Outward finger whip (Protective Parries); heel-of-palm downward (Hooking Arms); or inward (Fist of Aggression).

Flexion – Bending the wrist to move to move the palm and open fingerpads towards the medial forearm, as the lateral wrist moves in the opposite direction. The application intention could also be in either direction with various weapon options.

Examples: Upward 5-finger strike (Circling the Club); outward back-of-wrist strike (Calming the Club).

Radial Flexion – When the wrist bends (flexes) moving the thumb towards the radius bone (wrist bone on thumb side). Most commonly used to apply and handsword/karate chop using the meaty portion of the hand proximal to the little finger towards the target, but the thumb side can also be used to strike or hook.

Examples: Handsword out (Delayed Hand); handsword down (Six Hands); radius side wrist strike (Gripping Wrist).

Ulnar Flexion – When the wrist bends (flexes), moving the little finger towards the ulna bone (wrist bone on little finger side). This motion can be used in either direction as well where the thumb side can strike (reverse handsword and ridgehand strike) and the little finger side can strike and/or hook.

Examples: Reverse handsword strike up into the groin (Entangled Arm B); Upward reverse hammerfist (Circling the Arm); hooking the elbow crease causing it to bend (Triggered Palm); or the neck (Detouring the Kick.

Fingers/Hand: Closed - Open
The motion of closing the hand or using the closed hand and also opening the hand or using an already open hand.

Closing the Hand – Used to grab/grasp clothing or body parts to hold, or pinch muscles, tendons, nerve centers, skin, etc.

Examples: Grabbing (Crossing Grab), Pinching (Pinch from Death).

Closed Hand – The closed hand/fist is a primary martial arts weapon with flexibility for blunt force punching or as a hammering tool and can be formed into more refined shapes using various knuckles.

Examples: Punching (Crossing Fist); backknuckle (Alternating Fist); hammerfist (Lock of Death); reverse hammerfist (Circling the Arm). A single middle knuckle extended from a closed fist (Flashing Fist); all four second finger knuckles forming the half-fist (Pursuing Panther); or an inward knocking punch (Cradling the Baby).

Opening the Hand – Used to release a grip or moving to an open hand strike from a closed hand.

Examples: Letting go after manipulating (Bear and the Ram); opening the fingers to outward finger whip (Protective Parries).

Open Hand – A flexible weapon able to be formed open for use in many ways.

Examples: Handsword (Hand of Destruction); reverse handsword (Hand and Shield); palm strike (Thrusting Palm); heel-of-palm (Snapping Arm); back of wrist (Calming the Club); finger pokes (Thrusting Blade), finger slices (Turning Windmills); or just a slap (Tripping Leg).

The Leg: Hip - Knee - Ankle - Toes
<u>*Hip: Forward & Backward Leg Swing – In & Out Leg Circle – In & Out Hip Rotation*</u>**:** The leg hinging at the hip as one unit, like a pendulum.

Forward & Backward Leg Swing – A full leg movement where the entire leg is lifted in front or to the rear, with the reverse motion also have value.

Examples: Upward front kick (Buckling the Leg); outward ax kick (Circling the Kick B); stiff-leg lifting rear kick (Protective Circles); downward roundhouse ball kick (Broken Kneel).

Inward & Outward Leg Circle – Leg movements where the foot and lower leg follow an arc that travels inward towards the centerline or outward away from that centerline. An isolated motion without hip rotation is described here.

Examples: Outward ax kick (Gripping Wrist); pulling leg sweep (Glancing Poke).

Inward & Outward Hip Rotation – Leg movements in the middle of a kinetic kicking chain where the leg/foot is turned inward or outward off the hip to add acceleration and align weapon surfaces.

Examples: Roundhouse kick (Reversing Fist); inverted roundhouse kick (Dancing in the Dark); TSK pushing forwards after inverted rotation (Deflecting Pendulum).

<u>*Knee: Heel Lift Rear– Foot/Shin Front Extension*</u>
Bending the knee to lift the heel towards the rear of the body or lifting the bent knee in front where it can act as a hinge to extend the lower leg.

Heel Lift Examples: Upward heel kick (Retreating Pendulum), upward scoop kick (Sweeping the Leg).

Foot/Shin Examples: Kicks forward (Delayed Hand), upward (Parrying Grab), downward (Broken Kneel), and round (Reversing Fist).

<u>*Ankle: Extension – Flexion*</u>
The foot used either with or after the ankle has been bent (flexed) or straightened (extended) and always with appropriate foot position (*Toes*).

Ankle Extension – Ankle straightens (plantar flexion) toes away from shin.

Example: Front push-kick (Parrying Grab).

Ankle Flexion – Ankle bends (dorsiflexion) foot towards shin.

Examples: Inverted pulling sweep (Clipping Blade); front scoop kick (Destructive Circles).

<u>*Toes: Extension – Flexion*</u>
Toes form a contact surface or contribute to foot integrity for kicking.

Toe Extension – Pushing the toes, pointing them away from the foot.

Examples: Front push kick (Darting Fist); upward front kick (Hammerlock).

Toe Flexion – Pulling the toes, lifting towards top of foot (ball kick shape).

Example: Front snap kick (Delayed Hand).

Alignment of Muscular Force
This is how the physical structure aligns to generate force through and at the end of primarily an arm or leg motion. Two forces utilized by the muscle structure are *Pushing* or *Pulling* which, depending on the range of motion (ROM), are done in any *Direction of Motion*, along either *Path of Motion* although generally initiated along a linear path (see *Torque* to differentiate), at any *Angle of Motion*, or into any *Dimension of Motion*.

These motions use any of the *Point of Contact Variables* for striking or grappling where they can be linked, meaning that a pulling motion may begin with pushing (Taming the Fist) and vice versa (Jamming the Tackle).

It helps to understand the two sides of the body's *coronal plane* and how the front (anterior) and back (posterior) torso muscle structures have distinct roles in this process. Whether pushing or pulling the arms strongest starting point is with the elbow(s) on the front side of the body and close to, or connected with, the sides of our torso next to our ribs.

This position attaches the arms to the torso giving the hands and forearms muscular leverage, along with a springboard or rebounding surface to accelerate from, while also providing rib and torso protection.

If the elbow(s) start(s) behind the body to move forward not only is the front of the body exposed but the shoulder structure is in a weakened position that would require an additional motion to get the elbow(s) to the stronger forward, i.e. front of the body, position.

Note: The intention behind any muscular motion is important as a forward pushing motion is the same one used to pull something forward from behind (Crossed Arms) and in the other direction a pulling motion can be used to push something backwards (Captured Arms).

The upper and lower body will often be used together as complimentary *Pushing* and/or *Pulling* motions to influence different height zones on an opponent. This can especially be seen in stand-up grappling movements such as trips, throws, and takedowns.

Pushing
Pushing with the arms is primarily done forward (anterior coronal plane), away from the body, although rear arm pushing can also be done (Crashing Elbows). A stronger structure like the legs can push more powerfully, but generally with less dexterity.

The Arm: Forward - Across - Up - Down
Engaging the chest (pecs), shoulder (deltoids), and arm (triceps) muscles to move the hands and arms away from the body. This generally starts with a bent elbow before accelerating strikes or after connecting with or attaching to an opponent.

Forward – Motion where the hands are moved forward from the torso.

Examples: Straight punch (Crossing Fist); palm strike (Thrusting Palm); forward thumb strike (Thrusting Thumbs).

Across – Inward pushing motion travelling towards our own centerline.

Examples: Fingers-in palm strike (Tripping Leg); roundhouse punch (Darting Fist); whipping overhead punch (Flashing Fist).

Up – A motion that moves from low to high towards the front or rear.

Examples: Uppercut punch (Shielding Fingers); obscure elbow (Hidden Elbow); stiff-arm lifting punch (Spiraling Wrist).

Down – A motion from high to low in front of our own frontal plane.

Examples: Downward heel-of-palm (Hooking Arms); hairpin punch (Rear Belt Grab).

The Leg: Forward – Side – Rear
Engaging the hips (glutes, hip flexors, lower abs), upper (quads & hamstrings) and lower legs (calf, ankle, toes) to move the leg/foot away from the body to the front, side, or rear.

Forward – The straight leg (hip flexor, lower abs) or bent knee lifted in front from where the foot can extend (quadriceps) as the knee straightens to move the foot towards the front.

Examples: Upward front kick (Buckling the Leg); front push kick (Parrying Grab).

Side – The bent knee lifted in front, the same as when moving the foot forward, but the foot is then extended sideways.

Examples: Side snap kick (Twins of Aggression); side thrust kick (Buckling the Leg).

Rear – The straight leg lifted in back (glutes) or the bent knee lifting the heel towards the rear (hamstrings), or the foot then extended backwards as the leg straightens (glutes & hamstrings).

Examples: Stiff-leg lifting rear kick (Protective Circles); outer reap takedown (Sleeper); rear sliding leg sweep (Sweeping the Leg), rear thrust kick (Kick into Darkness).

Pulling
Pulling with the arms is primarily done moving the hands and arms towards the body from in front, although pulling can be used from rear to front (Crossed Arms). The legs can also be used to pull for some specialty purposes (i.e. rear scoop kick).

The Arm: Back – Up – Down
Moves primarily engaging the back (lats), shoulder (deltoids), and arm (biceps) muscles to move the hands and arms closer to our torso.

Back – Any type of clinch, hug, hold, or accelerated motion where the hands move towards and possibly behind the body. This includes ways that hold and hook the limbs or body at different heights and angles.

Examples: Frictional pull hooking down onto the forearms (Hooking Arms); pulling an opponent by his hand into a knee kick (Destructive Gift); pulling an opponent's body into a knee kick (Blinding Vice)

Up – Using the hand(s) and arm(s) from a lower level to a higher one to manipulate and control.

Examples: Pulling an opponent's head down as part of throw (Rolling Fists); pulling up on the arm to engage a stomp more effectively (Tripping Leg); grabbing then pulling up on the chin from behind a face down opponent (Leap of Death).

Down – Using the hand(s) and arm(s) from a higher level to a lower one to manipulate and control.

Examples: Grabbing the arm to pull down to cancel height and set up a strike (Flashing Fist); holding an opponent's head with a reverse head lock for pulling down onto an upward knee kick (Sweeping the Leg).

The Leg: Forward – Rear
Forward – Moving the foot and/or knee from the rear to the front with emphasis on the pulling aspect of the motion.

Example: Front pulling sweep to split the legs (Untwirling Pendulum).

Rear – Moving the foot and/or knee from the front to the rear of the body, also with emphasis on the pulling aspect of the motion.

Examples: Inverted sweep (Clipping the Blade); front scoop kick lifts in front then moves to the rear (Scraping Stomp).

Characteristics of Acceleration:
The focused intention of a movement as it travels through space or upon contact with a target based upon the return speed and entry/exit direction. These striking motions can retract or rebound after contacting a target surface or change to an alternate path/target after contact. The four methods are to *Thrust, Snap, Hook,* and *Whip*.

Thrust – Linear or Circular strikes that use body weight to drive and apply a heavy penetrating force onto and perhaps deep into a target before retracting along the same path. If followed by another strike then these are generally followed by another limbs weapon since this force is dispersed on the target unless reaccelerating on a different path of motion.

Examples: Straight palm strike lifts an opponent's head (Thrusting Palm); straight thrust punch penetrates the ribs (Crossing Fist); a side thrust kick buckles a knee (Buckling the Leg); same weapon arm trap down followed by upward elbow (Circling Elbow).

Snap – Linear or Circular strikes that rebound or bounce off a target surface quickly returning along the same path as delivered. Circular applications of this characteristic can also whip in route to the target but are differentiated by the return path, e.g. an outward snapping backknuckle returns along same path vs an outward whipping backknuckle that returns along a different path.

Examples: Inverted horizontal snap punch (Raking Fist); front snap kick (Delayed Hand), outward snapping backknuckle (Alternating Fist).

Hook – Circular motions of the arms and legs that connect at the apex of a circle or along the return path of a circular motion contracting towards the body center, then can retract along the same path or continue inwards to another position. These move from smaller to larger muscle groups and joints in a progression that compounds the strength to impact as the hands/arms contract towards the chest with the feet/legs contracting towards the glutes.

Arm Examples: Inward hook punch (Entangled Arm B), inward hooking backknuckle (Twirling Fist).

Leg Examples: Out hook kick (Thrusting Palm), up hook kick (Retreating Pendulum).

Whip – Circular motions of the arms and legs that connect at the apex the motions extension then returns along a different path, tracing an elliptical orbit. These move from larger to smaller muscle groups and joints in a progression that continuously increases the acceleration to impact where more acceleration is gained by shortening the circle while continuing through the target on a different path.

Arm Examples: Outward whipping backknuckle glancing through the temple hits at the extension apex (Hooking Arms); downward whipping backknuckle hits at the apex (Thundering Fists).

Leg Examples: Outward (Defending Cross) and inward crescent kicks (Darting Fist) hit at the extension apex. The Front (Unrolling Crane) kick (Sweeping the Leg) is unique in that it hits at and then after the extension apex sliding/scraping through a target after contact.

Point of Contact Variables

The three primary intentions used to affect a target are *Impact, Connect,* and *Attach. Impact* refers to accelerated moves that strike, hit, collide, or crash into a surface; *Connect* are moves that stick, slide, or check on a surface; *Attach* are body controlling moves that grasp, grab, and grapple after holding body areas.

Each contain sub-methods and can be used interactively in conjunction with, prior too, or following one of the other methods. Refer to the *Basics* chapter in the *Body* for a full list of methods.

Impact *(Accelerated Contact)* – Penetrating movements, however applied, that explode onto and perhaps into a target surface to break, crush, smash, knockout, takedown, tackle, or puncture. Associated terms include blocking, striking, punching, kicking, hitting, slapping, poking, bumping, tackling, pushing, shoving, etc.

These are generally done using the hands, elbows, knees, or feet for offensive and defensive purposes, with other body parts such as the head and even the entire body able to be used.

Connect *(Surface Contact)* – The connection or feel on a target or body surface after initial surface contact. This is done to monitor, transition, control, affect posture and/or position, or damage surface tissue. Associated terms include sliding, pressing, vibrating, checking, pinning, rubbing, scraping, sticking, tracking, touching, feeling, raking, etc.

They are done mostly with the hands, arms, shoulders, hips and/or legs. The two main category headings are to *Stick* in one area or *Slide* along a surface from one area to another which contains several sub-categories.

Stick – Maintaining contact onto a target surface. This often follows an *Impact* where it can check body position or attack sensitive points and be used as an *Attach* transition.

Examples: Four-finger poke after a palm strike (Six Hands); shoulder line cross-body check (Buckling Leg); forearm to elbow joint pressure (Crossing Grab); downward elbow check after downward elbow strike (Crossed Arms).

Slide – Moving along a target surface after initial contact. This often follows a *Stick* or *Impact* where it can then slice, claw, rake, rub, glance, or track a surface by following body contours.

Examples: Frictional pull along the forearms draws weight forward (Twin Lapel Grab); feeling along the arm to find & grasp the wrist (Crossing Fist).

Slice – Tracks surface contours tearing and ripping tissue by digging in with the fingernails side to side (Turning Windmills) or pulling to scrape (Hooking Arms).

Rake – Secondary attack by a different weapon on the same target surface after initial contact. The individual knuckles of the closed fist either inward (Raking Fist), or outward (Entwined Fist).

Glance – A combination method where a different surface is struck with the same or different weapon after initial contact. It is done as a prefix on the way to a primary target (Six Hands), or follow-up after impacting a primary target surface (Darting Fist).

Rub – Pressure into a sensitive area after initial contact by moving back and forth across tissue to stimulate and cause irritation. This is a common *Pressure Point* attack method whether to a limb (Obstructing the Club) or the torso (Grabbing Hair).

Attach *(Manipulation Contact)* – Movements supported within our own body structure and/or interlocked with an opponent. Associated terms include grasping, grabbing, grappling, locking, stretching, twisting, holding, hooking, pinching, squeezing, pulling, etc. Once attached these are used to hold someone in place for control, pain compliance, submission, or to move and manipulate their body.

Techniques would include grabbing with the hands (Crossing Fist), pinching with fingers (Pinch from Death), applying locks (Crossing Grab) and chokes (Turn of Fate), or other grappling maneuvers and holds.

These *Impact-Attach-Connect* Principles become more interactive when combined giving *Impact* (A), *Connect* (B), *Attach* (C) the following 12 sequential formulation variables, A-B; A-C; A-B-C; A-C-B; B-C; B-A; B-C-A; B-A-C; C-A; C-B; C-A-B; C-B-A.

These 12 *Impact-Connect-Attach* sequential variables include the possible ways to arrange all three methods, without interrupting the flow, repeating, alternating, or using them simultaneously, which would then make for an unlimited number of variables. For simplification only the six two-group methods of A-B; A-C; B-C; B-A; C-A; C-B are explained below.

Impact (A) then Connect (B) – Striking with then pressing a forearm against a throat into a wall to hold or collapse the trachea (Taming Fist), a palm strike to the face that stays connected to assist in a takedown (Crossed Arms).

Impact (A) then Attach (C) – Striking the radial arm nerve of an attacking knife hand then grasping the wrist for control (Thrusting Blade).

Connect (B) then Attach (C) – Pressing a cross body check across the chest followed by grabbing the clothes and/or pec muscles (Entwined Fist).

Connect (B) then Impact (A) – Sliding along an arm after hooking it into a heel palm strike (Destructive Circles) or sliding the foot along a shin in route to stomping a foot (Scraping Stomp).

Attach (C) then Impact (A) – A neck hook helps drive the head down onto an upward knee kick (Gripping Wrist) or grabbing the arm and wrist to guide the body into a front kick (Spiraling Wrist).

Attach (C) then Connect (B) – This sequence makes *Pressure Point* location less difficult. A crab-pinch around the throat then pushes and holds against a wall (Conquering Arm) or drives a head to the floor (Securing the Club).

States of Matter
This Ed Parker analogy provides motion characteristics to technique and movement analysis. It relates the *States of Matter, Solid, Liquid,* and *Gas* to describe *States of Motion.*

These *States of Matter* can also metaphorically relate to other Kenpo concepts such as the three *Stages of Learning (Primitive, Mechanical, Spontaneous)* and the three *Phases of Learning (Ideal, What If, Formulation).* The fourth *State of Matter, Plasma,* is added here.

Solid Motion – Solid maintains its structure and seeks its stature so this would refer to positions of movement and the space they occupy.

This can also relate to hard or linear styles of martial arts with strong solid stances and postures. The image of a practitioner in a wide, low, strong forward stance with a straight punch and opposite hand chambered as done in many Japanese "hard styles" shows this type of movement.

Liquid Motion – Liquid seeks its level, so this describes moves that flow around obstacles or fit efficiently into attack and defensive open spaces. It also relates to soft or circular styles of martial arts with unpredictable fluid circular motions and footwork. The image of a practitioner who continually shifts his weight with hands mimicking animals or complicated patterns as done by many Chinese "soft styles" shows this type of movement.

Gaseous Motion – Gas seeks its volume so this refers to utilizing complex compounded movements that can attack into many directions, levels, zones, and multiple targets simultaneously.

This refers to hard/soft movement styles, like Kenpo, that connect linear to circular and circular to linear while trying to utilize the best of *hard* and *soft* in fluid combinations that absorb into the allowable space, available angles, and uninhibited dimensions.

Examples: Scoop kick the groin with a palm strike to the sternum while simultaneously clawing the face (Unrolling Crane), rear sliding leg sweep with a hammerfist to the groin and a simultaneous opposite hand eye poke (Hand of Destruction).

Note: Gas is best utilized with temperature, pressure, and volume. Metaphorically, this is motivation, acceleration, and extension. *Motivation* is the temperature, intensity, and determination of our action; *Pressure* is the amount of force generated in the allowable space; *Extension* is the space covered within body dimensions.

Plasma – This is the explosion that happens when heat meets gas, creating the electrically conductive environment that makes fire, lightning, neon, and electric lights. This would be the explosion that occurs when a dynamic weapon meets and overwhelms a target, regardless of motion style.

Universal Pattern:
Another of Ed Parker's contributions to Kenpo and martial arts is what he created and called the *Universal Pattern*. This three-dimensional pattern shows the lines, circles, shapes, and paths of motion. Read Ed Parker's *Infinite Insights* book 1 for his description and analysis of his concept.

Included are his illustration and another to help clarify some of his concept.

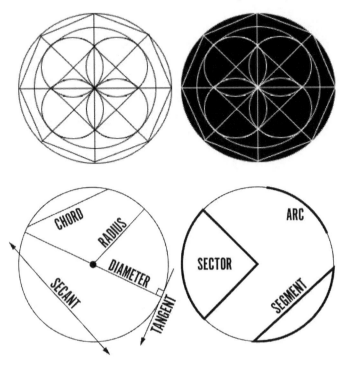

MUSCLE/MOVEMENT (MUSCLE) PRELOAD

This is the "potential energy" loaded into the musculoskeletal structure before it is used. This energy potential is strongest when primed by aligning the muscle structure for the next desired motion, or by moving from one *point of origin* into another logical and primed *point of origin*.

Powerful and efficiently connected arm motions are accelerated from the ground, through the legs, and into the accumulated leverage of the hips and rotation of the torso. The elbows can then reconnect with the torso, or the arms can brush each other when passing to reengage with the core muscles of the body for maximum acceleration and strength when applying a movement.

Aligning the body structure so muscles are stimulated and primed, i.e. preloaded, is how they engage and flex prior to use. Finding the most efficient way to do this is a skill level that usually requires instruction to attain. Since muscles work in pairs when one is contracted its complimentary muscle is relaxed, with its next action now preloaded in the relaxed muscle.

Note: Athlete's preparing for contact stimulate or prepare their muscles for motion and impact by stretching, flexing, cocking, winding up, rehearsing/repping, slapping, patting, etc. These are akin to how a cat prepares to move by stretching and crouching or an athlete slapping their muscles. Kenpo has these muscle stimulation slaps built into the technique flow, along with for timing, trapping, and rebounding reasons.

Bending the elbows while externally rotating the hand, i.e. palm up, pulls the elbows against the torso using the lat muscles and contracts the biceps, thereby preloading the arms for extension and internal hand rotation. That then relaxes the opposite side of those muscle groups to repeat this action if needed.

This preloading of muscles can be seen in sports such as baseball where a batter takes a few practice swings (rehearsing) then cocks (preloads) his bat and body before executing a powerful swing. A fielder bends his legs in preparation for movement and a pitcher winds up his body to gain velocity at the end of his hand when throwing the ball.

In the fighting disciplines this preload must be more subtle with the intended motion generally not telegraphed. Sophisticated martial art styles use, or are prepared to use, preloaded muscle groups through postures and sequential connections. The fighting stance with both hands up and palms facing each other illustrated here is preloaded for pushing or pulling.

A Boxer efficiently transitions from one preloaded position to another through practice and intelligent design of pre-formulated and drilled combinations. When his lead hand jabs, his rear hand is preloaded next to his chin, and when his rear hand punches, his lead hand is loaded to punch, often with a body maneuver, footwork, or a weight shift.

My daughter Jessica showing multiple *Preloaded* muscle groups as used in sport fighting and street defense, both ready to strike and resist pressure

In a street style, like Kenpo, these fighting positions are also not telegraphed from a *point of origin and* can be any natural posture since every position of the body preloads another position. These are practiced through intelligently designed patterns of attack and defense, called *Self-Defense Techniques* in Kenpo. These anticipate position and reaction while maximizing muscle preload.

These patterns account for every angle, range, and position of fighting while analyzing and practicing on live bodies, and eventually leading to random attack scenarios. This develops awareness and muscle memory to react without conscious thought to the stimulus of different attacks.

Like any sophisticated fighting system, Kenpo sets up an opponent towards a final result. This muscle preload, or potential energy, is best used when not obvious as a live opponent will adjust intentionally, reflexively, or instinctively.

I once heard someone expressing why they didn't like arts that teach sophisticated movement patterns, like Kenpo, and how happy they were learning a *one movement at a time* art because someone told them to keep it simple when fighting. Simplicity can be powerful and is often good enough, but a skilled single, or multiple opponent fight, can test and push the limits of simplicity. Besides, the skilled make the complex seem simple.

A skilled boxer or Kenpo practitioner uses many levels and layers to win a fight. Among these is preparing the next weapon to attack from the best position (i.e., angle and alignment), in the most efficient manner possible using muscle preload. What may seem like a simple combination of movements contains a high degree of sophistication (Fatal Variation).

Understanding this also enables recognition and anticipation of an opponent's intention, direction, and the power potential built into their posture and position. Recognizing preload, or lack of it, can be used against another person by assessing their body posture to expose weak muscle angles and positions.

If for example an opponent's palms are facing towards his face then their pushing muscles would be weaker making their hands are more easily pushed. Similarly, if their palms were facing away towards us then their pulling muscles would be weaker, so their hands are more easily pulled. This applies to every muscle group in the body.

Developing an educated awareness of muscle structure in the body for fighting can be developed using different methods. One of the more popular methods used in traditional martial art styles is the *Training Horse Stance* (see *Posture*).

Martial art masters developed and continue to have their students do this stance. Among many reasons is the development of overall body strength by pre-loading all the major and most minor muscle groups.

Contrary to ignorant opinions that this stance is a useless exercise position unrelated to fighting there are many subtleties and benefits to be gained through its practice. From the ground up:

Feet flat with toes turned forward or slightly inward grabbing the ground develops the minds connection with the ground through the feet along with building the muscular strength in the toes, feet, and ankles, while also helping develop the arches for explosive acceleration and stretching the Achilles tendon.

The angles of the feet pointed forward to slightly inward engage the vastus medialis (inside quadricep/thigh muscle) which is the first muscle that fires in the quadriceps muscle activation chain.

Sitting with knees bent preloads the legs at the tibialis anterior (shin muscles), stretches the gastrocnemius and soleus (calf muscles), prepares and develops the quadriceps and hamstrings (front and back thigh muscles), and the glutes (butt muscles), all of which are needed for an accelerated push off the feet and for building lower body core strength.

Pushing the knees out slightly adds to preload tension accumulated in the calf muscles along with developing muscle preload in the lateral ankle tendons and ligaments, all needed for springloaded acceleration. The adductors (muscles that pull the legs together) and abductors (muscles that push the legs apart) are also preloaded and strengthened.

Pushing the hips forward flattens the lower back (lumbo-sacral area), relieving back pressure while stretching the hip flexors for contraction and increasing the preload on the glutes while stabilizing the lower abdominal core. These are at the root of explosive lower body movement.

Pulling hands back to the waist (chamber position) with fists closed and palms up strengthens the grip and preloads the forearms for rotation. The biceps (pulling muscles) with the triceps (pushing muscles) and the four rotator cuff muscles are all flexed or "pre-loaded" along with the deltoids (shoulders), trapezius (upper back), latisimus dorsi (side of back), and pectoralis (chest) muscles.

The square symmetry of the horse stance position allows for working both sides of the body equally. This muscle balancing is important for coordination and developing bi-lateral and balanced muscular strength.

Other benefits include increased awareness of each foots position on the floor and points of acceleration from the bottoms of the feet (See *Balance*). An erect posture is important for spine health and efficient powerful whole-body movement (See *Posture*).

Whatever technique development is needed, or the athletic purpose used, and especially in the fighting disciplines, the study of muscle preload in our self and others can provide great insight into fully understanding how the human body can be applied as an offensive weapon or defensive tool.

MUSCULAR ACCELERATION

This describes how natural or man-made weapons are moved towards a target using the musculoskeletal structure. These are generally followed by a retraction, i.e. reverse motion, and are often a component of *Wave Transference* energy where an efficient muscle twitch results in a continuously accelerating linkage of muscular explosions aligned for maximum penetration upon contact.

This involves large and small muscles engaging to where the intention at the point of contact can be to thrust deep into and through a target or snap back from it. The intention of these is expressed in the old Kenpo saying that "you can snap a thrust, but you can't thrust a snap."

A linear thrust motion, like a rear kick, can also snap back (Kick into Darkness). Snapping movements, like the backknuckle strike or modified "flip" wheel kick, bounce, or rebound off their targets.

Example: *Thrusting* is a striking attitude where the weapon (often a soft collapsible target) hits then sticks and pushes deep into a target utilizing body/backup mass. It doesn't use the instant snapping retraction to reload as it was used to create space (Parting Arms) or due to some follow up with another weapon of the same limb (Hooking Arms) or as part of a different limbs application allowing for more time to influence and use a target for manipulation (Hand and Shield) and/or to move that weapon for another use at a new *point of origin* (Crossing Fist).

Example: *Snapping* is another striking attitude where the weapon bounces off the surface of a target then returns along the same path to its *point of origin*. This is often done to more dense or hard boney surface areas that are more difficult to penetrate, like the temple (Alternating Fists).

One of the martial arts best kept secrets for applying this *Muscular Acceleration* principle is the *Muscle Preload* discussed previously. Sophisticated fighting systems hide this in their postures and motions while using this knowledge to read an opponent's vulnerability based upon their body posture, position, and observed muscular alignment.

Example: Reading an opponent's movement to slip his cross punch with a lead hand inward block/catch then opposite hand straight punch followed by a same side kick/knee then an inward arm break utilizing the original blocking hand (Crossing Fist) utilizes Muscular Acceleration with *Muscle Preload* and *Wave Transference*.

Small motions also add to a movements overall muscular acceleration potential through this transference and pre-load.

Example: The wrist flexion at the end of a rear arm swing (Crushing Palm) or the internal forearm rotation used to accelerate an upward forearm strike (Fatal Variation).

WHIPPING ACCELERATION

A striking attitude used to apply circular hand and foot weapons which visually sounds like opening while applying larger to smaller joints and muscles away from the body center, however the human body can also apply this motion towards the body center with a spiraling shape.

However applied, this greatly builds acceleration to accumulate at the end point of a hand or foot weapon. It is rooted in *Wave Transference* and enhanced by *Torque and Rotation* where it can be applied at the apex then bounce back to its point of origin with a *snap* or by following a different path hitting after the apex with a *hook* or through the apex with a *whip*, i.e. Characteristics of Acceleration.

These choices at the extended circle's apex make for options depending on intent, body position, weight, and needed follow ups. Whether bouncing off to return to the point of origin with a snap or extended before traveling inward to hit after the apex with a hook (Long Form 2 Techniques #3 & 4) this whipping motion increases acceleration.

The greatest acceleration however, and the biggest "whipping motion" felt, hits at the apex where it then changes direction by shortening the circle to apply an elliptical orbit. This strike then slices through a target as it changes direction (Ascending from Death). This motion is generally done outward away from the body with the arms (Thundering Fists) or legs (Defending Cross) unraveling as it accumulates power, although spiraling inwards to the body with a progressively smaller and faster circle can be done (Snapping Arm) as can whipping forward (Untwirling Pendulum).

Example: Outward Whip-Snap – From a *forward bow* stance with a rear hand punch, then adjusting to a neutral bow launching a snapping backknuckle strike (Alternating Fist).

Example: Outward Whip-Thru – Inward elbow strikes the face then reverse motion the arm outward whipping an outward backknuckle strike through the opposite side of the same target area (Triggered Palm).

Example: Inward Whip-Spiral – An extended hammerfist rakes the nose inward followed an inward elbow strike (Snapping Arm).

Example: Inward Whip – After inward chest elbow then *outward finger whip* through one eye, use reverse motion with an inward finger whip through the other eye (Protective Parries).

Example: Forward Whip – The heel of a *rear scoop kick* is lifted into the groin then pulls and scrapes through the target by pulling the knee forwards (Untwirling Pendulum).

SPRINGLOADING

Using our structure through an internal, body surface, or external connection to build and store potential energy prior to a rapidly accelerating and explosive outward action. Although this uses *muscle pre-load* it is slightly different in that the load has a platform to launch from or be accelerated off of. This is quite common in weapon arts but can also be applied within the empty-hand arts.

Connecting to our own structure to build potential energy can also be seen in a simple Kenpo standing or meditating horse stance where the right closed fist is pressed into a left open hand ("Law of the Fist and the Empty Hand"). This initial hand position in most Kenpo Forms stores *potential energy* by pressing the fist gently against the open hand.

The illustration here is from James Mitoses' 1945 book, "What is Self-Defense - Kenpo Jiu Jitsu" that shows this as a starting position for self-defense. This *springloaded* hand posture forms a strong wedge for defense while priming and preloading the torso muscles for action, all with the hands up asking/praying/pleading not to fight (read the book if you can find it to fully understand that reference).

This principle increases structural support and loads the body *internally* to explode outwardly. The Kenpo *Neutral Bow* fighting stance is also energized in this way but for movement in any direction. The word "neutral" can give the impression of passivity but in actuality it defines a dynamic stance full of potential springloaded energy.

Example: Clapping the palms together before lifting them up between a two-hand straight wrist grab. This increases the strength, force, and leverage in the hands by connecting them to the torso structure making it easier to lift the hands out of that grip (Begging Palms)

Example: From double inward temple punches, the arms potential energy can then collapse into forearm strikes around the jaw (Blinding Vice).

Example: The front hand placed or bounced off the front thigh provides a front hand launching platform to punch or backknuckle, or the toes pushing off the ground to start a kicks acceleration. This subtle weapon launching technique has been used by Karate sport fighters and some well-known former Boxing champions like Muhammad Ali and Larry Holmes.

Example: Using an external structure like the ground to bounce up from, perhaps after dropping a knee to the spine, to jump switch with a roundhouse kick to the head (Leap of Death). A wall can also be used as a launching platform (Crossing Fist).

WAVE TRANSFERENCE

The progressive and accumulative movement of more than one joint and muscle group through a purposeful path of motion. This energy transference *compounds* in the body like a *wave*, generally moving from larger body areas to smaller ones. Through this process, the accumulation and compounding of body force builds up in power to and through a point of impact as used in martial arts.

Sports medicine uses the term "kinetic chain" to describe a similar idea. I prefer the more fluid term "wave" as that is how it should feel in the body. Presuming a connection with the ground for leverage, large motions use the entire body in this way with the waist as the key rotational axis point. Smaller motions can also use this linking method to compound energy through the body into a target.

This does not necessarily have to involve *torque* or *whip* if done without limb extension, as in a shoulder bump to create space or a tackle. Extending the limbs from this buildup of body mass uses the two major downstream *wave* patterns of shoulder-elbow-wrist with the fingers added on some strikes, and hip-knee-ankle with the toe joints added on some kicks.

Example: An *outward whipping backknuckle strike* starts with an outward hip and torso rotation using the waist as the chest turns and shoulder joint opens aiming the elbow then straightening the arm as the fist rotates from a hammering angle to a backknuckle angle, or vice versa if applying a whipping hammerfist, and the wrist extends the knuckles onto the target, or flexes for the hammerfist (Triggered Palm).

Example: A *front push kick* utilizes the hip flexors and abdominal muscles to lift the knee while supporting the weight on the opposite leg followed by the kicking leg straightening to extend the foot as the hips push, then the ankle extends the ball of the foot into the target followed by the toes pushing into the target (Parrying Grab).

Use of this principle to fluidly transfer and compound energy through any path of motion is used to build and accelerate force into powerful movements that are then transferred with intention into a point of contact.

TORQUE & ROTATION

Torque is a moment of force done by the body or its parts that involves turning or twisting, following a circular *path of motion,* with *rotation* in this context utilizing several principles including torque, leverage, and momentum.

Torque occurs as the torso, legs, and/or arms turn to increase weapon acceleration into an impact, or to manipulate an opponent's body. In martial arts it is used to increase the impact speed of a muscular acceleration such as turning the hand when extending a straight punch or breaking someone's balance and posture by turning their wrist or both (Crossing Grab).

Large and small body movements can be used like the minor torso turn used to extend a jab or the rear heel turning over to help push the rear hip and shoulder forward helping to drive a rear hand punch forward. For most punches, a wrist rotation is also done which adds to the overall acceleration, compounding the torque. Locking movements are also constructed to generate torque on vulnerable tissue (Twisting the Gift).

The magnitude of torque depends on three quantities: 1) The muscular force applied to accelerate the torque; 2) the length of the lever arm connecting to the axis (joint) of the weapon; 3) and the angle created by them. These are the actual movement components referred to as "torque." With a fulcrum this becomes a type of *Mechanical Advantage*.

In its pure form each manifestation of torque can be looked at independently, but the reality is that these components of torque generally work simultaneously or in firing sequence. They compound through more than one lever arm as *Wave Transference* that culminates in a dynamic explosion of focused energy onto or into a target.

These moments of force can be seen in small muscle twitch actions like turning the forearms and hands palm up to help anchor the elbow and/or turning the hands palm down with the forearm lifting the elbow. These small twitch motions generate quick but powerful points of acceleration that are especially effective at close range (Fist of Aggression).

Another use would be the lateral flexion of the wrist used upon contact to apply a downward handsword strike (Charging Tackle) or the increased pressure applied where a reinforced arm choke is used to crush an opponent's jaw and face structure (Sweeping the Leg).

Rotation is the act of moving around an axis or central point so can happen at different places in the body. A whole-body motion where the body turns to one side then to the other, left to right and right to left, along with the winding/unwinding of the arms and legs at their ball and socket joints, or the coiling/uncoiling of all the bodies parts working together.

This *force couple* type of motion is limited by foot location and pivot point placement where a *forward bow* stance allows for less shoulder turning than a *close kneel* stance which allows for less shoulder turning than a *rotating twist* stance.

This back and forth action generates acceleration and force, especially in the arms for striking, as the opposite side is reloaded, or *preloaded*, by the previous strike (Thundering Fists).

Its force is generated and compounded using an agitator action, like inside a washing machine. This motion was the main martial art premise in the Karate Kid II movie where it was called the "drum technique" illustrated by the Japanese pellet drum.

This motion can be demonstrated by doing the simple and common exercise known as "trunk rotation" where the shoulders move one forward with the opposite moving back (i.e., reverse motion) then to the other side.
It is also usually done by shifting the weight towards one foot and pivoting the opposite now lighter foot heel up, then to the opposite side in an alternating manner usually with the arms bent so the opposite elbow alternates towards the weighted foot.

Another version of this exercise is done by Chi Gung practitioners where the feet are flat with the knees slightly bent with arms hanging down relaxed at the sides as the completely relaxed body is turned at the shoulders from one side to the other, allowing the arms to gently whip around contacting the front and rear body simultaneously at the end of each rotation, then rebounding to move in the opposite direction in an alternating manner. For health, these arm/hand taps can be directed to stimulate different parts (usually organs) of the body for energy at these various strategic locations.

Its use in martial arts is unique as the human body can apply these alternating motions with varying lever arm lengths such as hitting with an extended hand on one side followed by an elbow on the other (Hand and Shield). There are also components of "reverse" and "opposite" motions when doing this type of action (Ascending from Death).

Foot pivoting increases the rotational mass by adding momentum and inertia (Defying the Club). This can also be applied using an opponent's rotation to disrupt their balance by pushing and guiding their body (Piercing Blade) or used as the "spiralling staircase" analogy in Parker's terminology (Falling Eagle).

DROPPING/SETTLING

In Kenpo this is commonly termed "Marriage of Gravity" as coined by SGM Edmund K Parker. His original definition is, "the uniting of mind, breath and strength while simultaneously dropping your body weight along with the execution of your natural weapon(s)."

When the components of this dropping/settling body-weight are timed properly the force is increased as gravity aids to add weight and acceleration to any downward moving strike. This combined action literally causes a marriage with gravity by using vertical body momentum through the height dimension and is often coupled with the ground to sandwich a target as done extensively in Kenpo Form 5.

In Kenpo circles the original meaning is usually demonstrated with the technique called "Delayed Hand/Sword" where, after kicking an opponent in the groin, the foot settles to the ground with an outward handsword strike onto the side of their neck. This strike is done at a slightly downward diagonal angle as the weight settles with breath and mental intention.

Adding to this, I teach four ways the weight can settle using this principle. These are differentiated by striking angle and the footwork used to apply it. Along with the *Downward Diagonal* application in "Delayed Hand" there are also *Forward*, *Downward* and *Reverse Gravity* methods. This necessary principle is an important exception to the general movement tenet of keeping the head level.

Examples: Downward Diagonal – "Delayed Hand/Sword" is the standard example mentioned above but another is an inward elbow strike applied diagonally downward sandwiching through the jaw combined with an inward heel-of-palm strike (Raking Fist). The weight is also dropped in this way when doing a downward diagonal wheel kick (Reversing Fist).

Example: Forward – A straight vertical punch can be enhanced by adding a slightly downward trajectory upon contact by settling the weight as the punch hits. Anchoring the arm muscles slightly downward with ulnar wrist flexion drives the punching knuckles down making the punch heavier (Parting Arms).

Examples: Downward – As an opponent's head is pulled down onto an upward knee kick the closer to opponent arm circles into an overhead downward elbow as the foot settles and the weight drops (Sweeping the Leg), or anytime a knee is dropped onto a target (Evading the Club).

Examples: Reverse Gravity – Shifting the weight rapidly from foot to foot by lifting the weighted foot slightly, thereby allowing gravity to add downward weighted acceleration to the body (Thundering Fists). This is not done by jumping but by lifting the feet faster than the weight can drop. It can look like alternating or simultaneous stomping to the untrained eye and is often used to accelerate towards a new direction when using body *rotation* (Broken Kneel).

LIFTING/RISING

Moves where the force travels upward, with the energy produced able to apply force through targets that include an opponent's obscure zones, increasing its power and effectiveness.

The legs and core are generally what is used to explosively lift through a target to increase the force of these upward strikes or movements. A lower body prep or downward motion often precedes and/or follows this lifting up into a target.

An opponent can be either held in place, pulled down, or moved away to an extended range. Contact can be done in a straight *Vertical Line* upward or follow a *Diagonal Line* upward both using large and small body motions.

Example: Lifting Vertical Line – In defending a held guillotine choke, use tenderizing techniques until able to duck out from the choking arm and, while still holding onto that wrist, stand up with an obscure elbow strike under his chin while pulling down on his wrist to bring his head down, adding force to the upward lifting elbow strike (Locked Horns).

Example: Lifting Vertical Line – After creating a gap against a rear bear hug attack, stomp his foot causing his head to reflexively move down into an obscure elbow strike moving up under his chin, exposing his throat for an outward handsword strike (Captured Arms).

Example: Lifting Diagonal Line – From a bent position in front of an opponent after striking his inner knees with a closed fist, stand with an outward raking hammerfist across and through his nose or temple, which can initiate a multiple strike follow up (Entangled Arm B).

Example: Lifting Diagonal Line – After stepping behind a rear bear hug opponent, an elbow is lifted at a diagonal under his chin, lifting through the legs, before an opposite hand hammerfist is dropped downward diagonally onto his lower abdomen as the body settles (Crashing Elbows).

COLLAPSING/COMPRESSING

Moving from an expanded body position to a less expanded one, *Collapsing* or *Compressing* around a structure, such as sandwiching weapons around an opponent's body or part, and/or in preparation for *expanding*. This *collapsing* is often done after preloading with an *Expanding* motion, possibly in reflex to an attack, or as a way for the body to accelerate downward and/or inward. It can occur gradually or explosively depending on the method and target.

Areas of the torso, especially the groin and over internal organs, reflexively contract inward towards a threatened or damaged area, where attacking nerves causes a reflexive expansion outward from the attacked area. See *Pressure Point* chapter in the *Body*.

Collapsing weapons are used for *Choking, Squeezing, Holding, Pinching, Biting,* and *Sandwiching.*

Choking methods vary but all involve attacking the neck/throat area using various hand, arm, or leg techniques, with the objective to disrupt blood and/or airflow between the head and body (Turn of Fate). See *Choke/Chokehold* and *Strangle* in Vocabulary and Terminology Chapter.

Squeezing happens in choking for sure as it refers to closing the space inside of a hold where the muscle contraction becomes progressively tighter around the tissue, like an Anaconda continually tightening its grip around a prey but is also done doing bear-hugs and clinches (Blinding Vice).

Holding involves methods that use the hands, arms, or legs to control another person. Although not necessarily debilitating, it provides a way to control and avoid contact while manipulating, stalling, or maneuvering to another position (Parrying Grab).

Pinching is a grasping method applied using one of two primary techniques. They are the thumb/index pinch and four-finger "horsebite" pinch (no thumb) and both used to grasp and squeeze a small amount of skin, generally in a sensitive area of the body (inner thigh, inner bicep, upper chest, kidneys, etc. See *Basics* chapter in Body), to generate a nerve response (Pinch from Death).

Biting seems self-explanatory and is only acceptable in a potential life or death situation. It can be used to cause release of a hold where limb damage or unconsciousness is inevitable (Locked Horns), or the life or death carotid artery bite that, although repulsive, is and has been used in life or death struggles since the beginning of hand-to-hand combat.

Sandwiching are movements where two accelerated weapons collapse around a target (Lock of Death). An inward elbow to one side of the head simultaneously applied with an inward heel-of-palm strike to the other side of the head causes a violent compression that Kenpo people often call an "elbow smash" (Raking Fist). The ground is also a powerful sandwiching force that can be utilized (Twisted Gun).

EXPANDING

The body opening outward from a smaller contracted position to a larger more expanded one. This is done to create space within a hold or to attack as the body opens. It occurs from either a normal posture, or after preloading with a *Collapsing* motion, or in reaction to attack.

Something to observe in the body is that stimulated nerves react by expanding outward, moving away from the area under attack as in a *crossed extensor reflex*, whereas when the torso is injured it tends to collapse and contract around the traumatized area. See *Pressure Point* chapter in the *Body*.

Knowing this in ourselves helps us to know this in others so can be important in affecting an opponent's posture and in checking his reflex to any trauma that we may cause.

As an offensive tool this *Expanding* of the body and/or its parts is a powerful force we can use, generally with larger motions, to open up an area with our torso and/or strike with our limbs along that growing/expanding path. Like with most complimentary opposites, i.e. Yin/Yang, an expansion movement is often followed by a *Collapsing* movement (Locked Horns).

Example: Checking Expanding – Sweeping with one leg behind an opponent's leg could result in what is everyone's natural reaction to falling, backwards in this case, which is reaching back or grabbing onto a nearby support structure so using our arm to check/hold their same side arm eliminates that arm from becoming an unintentional weapon as they are driven to the ground (Deflecting Pendulum).

Example: Torso Expanding – If held in a rear bear hug with both arms pinned, and after any tenderizing techniques help cause a relaxation of the hold, explosively opening the arms and chest while turning the torso and flaring the elbows to help rotate and open them outwards, thereby creating space within the attacker's arms for maneuvering (Captured Arms).

Example: Limb Expanding – Both arms circling up and back against two attackers on either side of a shoulder grab, striking and clawing in that flow before wrapping around both of their arms prior into a powerful *Collapsing* inward return motion causing manipulation and possibly injury (Fingers of Wisdom).

REBOUNDING

Using our own body or that of an opponent to rebound/bounce off from thereby enabling our weapon to change direction instantly and gain acceleration rapidly towards another target or position.

This can be done off our own body to change a weapons direction, off our own body to return a weapon along the same path, off an opponent's body to rebound into another target on the same opponent, or from one opponent's body into another opponent.

Example: Our Own Body Change Direction Rebound – From a lead side inward elbow on an opponent's chest, rear hand checking their elbow and front knee checking their front knee, extend the elbow sides hand with an outward finger whip through his near eye then rebound/bounce the chambered elbow off your own side to launch an inward finger slice through his opposite eye (Protective Parries).

Example: Our Own Body Same Direction Rebound – After a rear side palm strike to an opponent's face that hand retracts, while applying a lead hand inverted punch to his solar plexus, to connect with our own lead side anterior chest/shoulder where it can rebound/bounce off to reaccelerate an outward handsword strike to the opponent's neck, making for a rapid-fire hand striking combination (Six Hands).

Example: Same Opponent Different Target Rebound – After a rear hand forward hammerfist to an opponent's groin, while checking his arms with our front hand, that hand then rebounds/bounces off his groin up to apply an outward backknuckle strike to the opponent's nose (Rolling Fists).

Example: Different Opponent Rebound – Against two attackers, one in front and one behind, a front kick to the front opponent bounces/rebounds off that front attacker to begin its acceleration into the second rear attacker with a rear thrust kick (Opposing Palms).

Note: Kenpo has been called a "slap art" by some watching it, often "in the air" where an ignorant and probably disdainful eye can get this perception. Aside from the fact that slapping is a useful method of striking, these "slaps" are many things in Kenpo including pinning checks, timing adjustments, muscle pre-load setups, body contact warmup stimulation, setups for defensive posture, and as methods of changing direction (i.e., *Rebounding*).

STRETCH REFLEX ACCELERATION

This physiological function within a muscle structure that happens after stretching where the elasticity in the muscle(s) makes them want to return to their natural and un-stretched position. This creates the potential for a rapidly accelerating return motion or kickback after muscles, tendons, and even ligaments or joints have been extended, stretched, or twisted.

This can occur as a return motion along the same path (i.e., *reverse motion*), as an alternate path after an extension motion, or by using the stretch reflex in an opponent's structure. It's like a slingshot where the load of one motion provides energy potential of another motion in the opposite direction.

Example: Same-Path Stretch Reflex – After standing up and out of a defended guillotine choke with a lead side obscure elbow strike under an opponent's chin, that arm then continues outward with a claw as the rear side hand checks by also moving outwards. Both motions together open the chest and shoulders, like a "chain-breaker" warm-up exercise.

The natural preloaded return contraction of the arms at this point towards our own centerline is then used, with intention, to apply a lead inward elbow strike with a rear hand inward heel-of-palm strike to sandwich the head, or staggered high/low on head targets to damage the neck (Locked Horns).

Example: Alternate-Path Stretch Reflex – A rear sliding leg sweep through the front of an opponent's knee not only causes his head to come forward and down (i.e., *Involuntary Momentum*), but our sweeping leg, after locking straight behind us in a reverse bow, then naturally wants to relax and those muscles release. This makes for a naturally accelerating upward knee kick into the opponent's face (Sweeping the Leg).

Example: Opponent's Structure Stretch Reflex – Wrapping our arm(s) up-back-around the bent elbow of one (Wraparound) or two (Fingers of Wisdom) attackers that are grabbing our shoulder(s) from the side, and then strongly locking and moving their arm(s) at their bent elbow(s) with our arm(s) to move them and perhaps damage their shoulder(s).

These stretched joints can then provide not only be used for manipulation but creates potential energy for a return point of acceleration with our own hand(s), (i.e., *Manipulated Involuntary Momentum*), as their body(s) adjust forward to relieve pressure on their elbows.

Note: This can also be used "in the air" to practice various movements, especially kicking. After extending a right front kick in one direction (10:30) the retraction motion can rapidly and naturally be redirected to become a right side thrust kick in another direction (1:30) and then be accelerated as a right wheel kick between the two (12) as done in "Kicking Set 2" (see *Sets* in the *Body*).

MAJOR & MINOR PRINCIPLE

Ed Parker originally defined the *Minor/Major Principle* as "the principle that a minor move, while subordinate and not devastating, can cause ample damage and/or delay the execution of a major move to occur. Major moves are strong and positive moves which cause immediate devastation."

This definition can be confusing when seen through real life applications because of the overlap between these two ideas of *Minor* being "not devastating" and *Major* causing "immediate devastation." This can leave the impression that a certain type of movement/motion is minor or major where defining the *Effect* or result of an applied movement would seem to be what would define the notion of this principle.

The reality is that a big "major" motion could have a small or even no effect on an opponent and a small simple "minor" motion could have a big effect on that same opponent.

Angle, depth of penetration, target to weapon match up, and intention, along with the mindset, durability, and resiliency of an opponent become factors when determining how to categorize a move using this Principle. This is all of course partially about the semantics of the words, but a clarification and expansion of the terms seems needed to make it all work.

Therefore, my explanation includes more possibilities as I am adding the notion of *Effect*. These are that *Major Moves* can cause a *Major* or a *Minor Effect* and *Minor Moves* can also have a *Major* or a *Minor Effect*. To address this and complete the definition I have added two categories that focus on the effect of the action applied.

Levels of Force provides the result reference needed to determine and delineate what is meant by *Effect* and the subtleties that take this from a *Concept* to a *Principle*. To review, the "Levels of Force" in order are: Distraction / Attention Getter; Control &/or Discomfort; Strain &/or Sprain; Break &/or Dislocate; Unconsciousness/Knockout; Disable; Death/Kill.

Major Move with a Minor Effect
These are large powerful movements that have a temporary effect on an opponent. A liver punch can stop someone from fighting but is most likely recoverable or might even be mentally pushed through by some as they stall while recovering. A side thrust kick to the back of a knee could buckle a knee but would most likely not disable an opponent. Both result in *Control & Discomfort* (Crossing Fist).

Major Move with a Major Effect
These are large powerful movements that break, crush, dislocate, rupture, or otherwise destroy the intended target. The previous side thrust kick if done to the side or front of the knee could *Break &/or Dislocate* the joint (Twins of Aggression), causing a debilitating more long-term injury.

More seriously, a handsword strike to the back of the neck or an elbow down onto the spine crushing the vertebrae could cause *Unconsciousness or Death* (Sweeping the Leg).

Minor Move with a Minor Effect
These are smaller or incidental movements to prevent an action, or whose effects stay within the first three "Levels of Force." Checking or parrying are typical minor movements used as defense or to setup another move that could possibly cause discomfort to an opponent.

Pinching is an example of a minor move having a minor affect. Done to a tender area this can affect an opponent's posture or cause a hold to be released (Pinch from Death).

Minor Move with a Major Effect
These are smaller movements that can have devastating results. A finger poke to the eye is a minor movement that can have a major effect on an attacker (Protective Parries).

An upward hook kick between the legs crushing the testicles against the pubic bone is another minor movement that can have a major effect (Crushing Palm).

Using these four possibilities as a baseline, the human component must also be considered and the reaction to action variables. A major factor, aside from our accuracy and intention, is the pain threshold and durability of the person being struck. The wide variation of pain tolerance and determination levels among people can create an overlap in this evaluation where one person can continue to fight with a broken arm while another would stop with a hammered bicep.

In a life or death situation people will fight until they cannot physically function where in a playground fight between 1st graders it may stop with one relatively minor punch or a hard block of that punch. It may also take several major moves to stop one attacker or one minor move to stop a another. As always, keep fighting until it really is over.

MECHANICAL ADVANTAGE

A group of methods used to increase force through the knowledge of body structure, body mechanics, gravity, and a little geometry. Described are *Structural Alignment, Structural Reinforcement,* and the shared engineering terms of *Leverage, Wedge,* and *Force Couple.*

Structural Alignment

Using individual or multiple musculoskeletal components stacked using nearby joints and muscles to form a straight line towards a target or weapon. These can be used as a brace to create space, maintain space, as a blocking surface to resist force, or as a powerful striking, pushing, or framing surface to overpower a target.

Perhaps the most powerful of these natural body alignments, when properly positioned, are the humerus bones of the upper arms and femur bones of the upper legs. Positioning the bent elbow(s) or knee(s) so they are pointed towards a target or weapon with the other end, connected to our body, directly behind forming a straight line like a battering ram is used extensively in martial arts.

Example: Offensive Punching – A jab is applied with a straight wrist (Radius next to Ulna bones), a straight but not hyper-extended elbow (humerus bone alignment), and the torso turned so the lead shoulder is in front of the rear shoulder (collar bones with sternum) all aligned to the rear foot connected on the ground (hip to femur to Tibia next to Fibula) in a strong line towards a target for punching leverage (Boxing Sparring #1).

Examples: Offensive Elbow – As a pushing surface the elbow tip can be pressed into an attacker's armpit (i.e., humerus alignment) to stop forward progress and injure (Protective Circles), break balance (Falling Eagle), or hit/press into the solar plexus to create space within a lock (Entangled Arm B).

Examples: Defensive Elbow – An extended outward block is best applied with hand rotated palm forward and slightly in front of the elbow (tricep engaged) with the elbow slightly outside the centerline (perpendicular to attack) with knees bent and the furthest foot on the ground all aligned with the arms application to provide leverage for the whole structure. This can be applied moving forward to jam (Securing the Club) or backward to absorb (Shielding Fingers).

Example: Defensive Knee – Defending a powerful roundhouse kick by using the same side knee and elbow together to form a wall that blocks the kick (Kickboxing Sparring #5). See *Sport Fighting* chapter in the *Body.*

Example: Combined Legs – The shin of one leg locked past and with the calf of the other over a trapped elbow (i.e., twist stance) provides a bracing frame for damaging the elbow (Twisted Gun).

Example: Combined Arms – An upward crossed block where one forearm connects with the other to form a strong connected structure for blocking (Obstructing the Club)

Examples: Combined Elbow and Knee – From a bottom side-mount grappling position with the elbow ends placed into the hip and neck or armpit to maintain space for breathing and maneuvering (Position Grappling Sparring #7); or from a top side-mount grappling position putting the bent knee onto an opponent's stomach pushing into his diaphragm (Position Grappling Sparring #3).

See *Sport Fighting* chapter in *Body* book for the referenced "Sparring Lists."

Structural Reinforcement
The use of one anatomical structure connected to another by using our own *self-contained structure*, the *opponent's structure*, and/or a *nearby structure/surface*. This provides resistance that reinforce a powerful attack, solidify a grip, resist oncoming force, brace a structure, or becomes a launching platform. This is common in standup and ground grappling to solidify and/or defend against a grip, lock, or hold.

Examples: Offensive Self-Contained Structure – Grabbing our own clothing after surrounding their arm (Wraparound); grabbing our other arm after surrounding their elbow joint (Securing the Club); placing one hand on top of the other to assist in pushing an opponent's arm down before launching an eye poke (Glancing Poke).

Examples: Defensive Self-Contained Structure – Connecting our forearms together while cross blocking upwards (Obstructing the Club); using one palm to support the other against a wristlock attack, with the forehead able to be added as additional reinforcement supporting the hand (Entangled Arm); placing the back of our overlapped hands against our own forehead to support our neck from the pressure of a full-nelson attempt, until a release can be affected (Scraping Stomp).

Examples: Opponent's Structure (isolated or against them self) – After countering a two-hand read choke by pinning the attacker's thumb(s) webbing against our neck then turning our shoulders to damage his thumb joint (isolated) while ducking out, followed by locking their elbows together (against them self) to apply pressure (Cross of Destruction); sitting back against the knee of a rear bear hug opponent then reaching under to grab and lift his foot forward between our legs, causing him to fall back (Straddling the Leg).

Examples: Nearby Surface – Using the forearm to press against an opponent's throat bracing and holding him against a wall (Taming the Fist); placing our hands on a wall to support while kicking (Turning Windmills); bracing our back against a wall while kicking (Conquering Arm), using another person (Bear and the Ram) behind us as a brace for delivering a kick forward (Bear and the Ram), or pinning the opponent to a wall (Crossing Fist).

Leverage

How force is applied (effort) at the end of a lever arm such as a leg, an arm, or the whole body around a pivot point (fulcrum) to magnify power that moves/impacts an object (load). This is used in martial arts to gain and apply a mechanical or structural advantage over an opponent and to utilize our own structure more effectively.

The 3 *Points on a Lever* are *Effort, Load,* and *Fulcrum,* of which "3 Classifications of Levers" can be configured. These are applied in the fighting disciplines through grappling and striking.

In grappling this leverage is constructed using the framework of interlocking limbs, along with torsos and the ground to immobilize structures under attack or being controlled.

Example: Grappling Leverage – Applying a rear naked sleeper choke using one arm around the throat (effort) connected to the other arm and attached to their head with the chest as a supportive expandable structure (all fulcrums) as the space is closed around the throat (load) to affect control and consciousness (Escaping Death).

In striking, this leverage is applied at the end of an accelerated movement, making the timing of each lever component important to generating force.

Example: Striking Leverage – As a rear hand punch (effort) hits a target (load) the ball of the rear foot on the ground (fulcrum) is simultaneously turned (Crossing Fist). This should also happen with the front hand as the force to either hand comes directly from the foot's connection with the ground on the same side (Alternating Fist).

Note: When teaching this concept of stepping with a punch, I find it best to have students exaggerate this movement at first by hitting the ground with the ball-of-foot simultaneously while punching a target, to where it looks like marching while punching. That is then refined as the body mechanics become more natural. This is where the saying "hand speed = foot speed" evolves and where heavy explosive punching/striking power is generated.

3 Points on a Lever: (E.L.F.)
Effort   (where the energy is exerted)
Load   (what is being moved or manipulated)
Fulcrum   (an anchored pivot point that provides stability)

3 Classifications of Levers:
Type 1 Lever - Fulcrum in the middle, Effort & Load on either end
A *one-arm* Type 1 Lever would be a pry bar, or any single lever arm, with one end placed under a large rock (load) while an area between the two ends is connected to the ground (fulcrum) with the free end able to be pushed downward (effort) to move the rock more easily. Another is a teeter-totter or see-saw where a child on each end alternate between effort and load around a middle pivot point (fulcrum).

Example: One-Arm Type 1 Lever – Bracing an opponent's elbow against our side while pulling their wrist to move them around us (Piercing Blade).

A *two-arm* Type 1 Lever would be a pair of scissors, connected in the middle (fulcrum), with force applied at the handles (effort), causing the two sharp blades to glide past each other (load).

Example: Two-Arm Type 1 Lever – This type of lever can be seen in an art like Judo where throws are used with the hip applied as a center pivot point (fulcrum), while the upper body is pulled (effort), to move the lower body (load) around the pivot point and to the ground (Eluding Death A).

Type 2 Lever - Load in the middle, Effort & Fulcrum on either end
A *one-arm* Type 2 lever would be a door (load), connected to a frame at the hinges (fulcrum), and opened at the knob (effort). A diving board is another example under this classification.

Examples: One-Arm Type 2 Lever – Circling an overhead downward handsword onto the back of the neck (Charging Tackle); Pulling the hand of a handshake attack, moving the arm and that side of their body forward, cancelling their opposite side punch (Destructive Gift).

A *two-arm* Type 2 lever is a nutcracker connected on one end (fulcrum), with the nut placed between the arms (load), and pressure applied at the free ends to crush the nut (effort).

Example: Two-Arm Type 2 Lever – This type of lever is seen in reaps, leg trips, sweeps, and takedowns where the leg(s) are braced and/or moved one way (fulcrum), while the upper body is pushed another way (effort), causing the body (load) to fall (Dance of Death).

Type 3 Lever - Effort in the middle, Load & Fulcrum on either end
A *one-arm* Type 3 lever would be a tongue depressor used by a doctor that is held on one end (fulcrum) while pressed in the middle (effort) to push and hold the tongue down (load).

Example: One-Arm Type 3 Lever – Applying a downward armbar where an opponent's wrist is anchored against our hip (fulcrum) while our forearm or hand presses against their elbow joint (effort) to move their body (load) in the desired direction (Obstructing the Club).

Note: Grappling moves, unlike striking movements, can create their own fulcrum within the body structure.

A *two-arm* Type 3 lever would be a pair of tweezers ("V" shaped version) connected on one end (fulcrum) with pressure applied in the middle (effort) to help the tweezers grab and remove a splinter (load).

Example: Two-Armed Type 3 Lever – This is the type of lever applied when punching or striking a target. The ground is the connecting point (fulcrum) for the body to accelerate (effort) so the punch or strike can be effective upon hitting a target (load) to damage tissue (Crossing Fist).

Notes: Boxing coaches often reference "punching with leverage" (Boxing Sparring #1-4). Also, missing a target when striking, or moving *in the air/shadowboxing,* results in no load being moved at the end of the extension. This then becomes a *Type 2 Lever* where the effort is the missed and the load becomes our own body.

Wedge
A two-arm lever forming a "V" shape to *Pry* open a narrow space, or a one-lever arm forming an "I" shape that can create an *Angle of Deflection.*

The "V" shape is like a doorstop placed into a small opening to progressively stop a doors movement, or a flock of geese cutting through the air.

Examples: "V" Shaped Wedge – Putting the hands together in a prayer position, then driving/prying this "V" lever shape up through the attacking forearms of a high two-hand wrist grab (Begging Palms) or push (Parting Arms) or choke (Blinding Vice).

The "I" shape is like a pry-bar pushed in-between two spaces to help create more space or as a deflecting surface like one side of an angled roof where rain and snow can slide down.

Examples: "I" Shaped Wedge – Pushing a single "I" lever arm up into a diagonal as done in an upward block (Evading the Club) or swinging an arm down diagonally as in a deflecting downward block (Deflecting Pendulum).

Force Couple
This mechanical engineering term refers to a free vector or lever arm freely moving or rotating at or around a connecting point independently of that connection. This can be a single limb hinging like the pendulum in an old clock or more than one arm rotating on either side of the connecting point like a helicopter blade spinning around its center.

On the human structure this is analogous to the arm hinging off the shoulder or leg hinging off the hip. It also refers to the shoulders and hips rotating the torso around the body centerline so as one side moves forward the other moves backwards.

These can all be enhanced with muscular force in martial arts for defensive or offensive use and is an unavoidable motion used in standup for striking with alternating hands (rotation) and when applying a push and/or pull of the body around a centerline. It can also be used with a scissoring effect.

Examples: Limb-Hinging Force Couple – Circling the straight arm overhead and down to strike onto a target with the hand (Charging Tackle) or elbow (Sweeping the Leg). The leg can be used as an ax kick (Alternating Fists).

Example: Combination Striking Force Couple – A lead side outward handsword followed by a rear side straight palm strike followed by a lead inverted punch followed by a rear side outward handsword strike that manipulates posture followed by a lead side downward handsword strike (Six Hands).

Example: Torso Rotation Force Couple – Having one shoulder pushed causing the other shoulder to accelerate forward (Triggered Palm) or pushing one side while pulling the other to turn an opponent (Turn of Fate).

Scissoring Force Couple Example: Trapping the arm between forward and backward motions can be used to scissor a joint for manipulation and/or to cause damage (Glancing Palm).

BORROWED FORCE

This principle uses an opponent's-initiated force against them. Their pulling force is most often used to define and apply this principle but pushing energy can also be used to generate increased power if around a *Force Couple*.

Example: Pulling – As the upper body is pulled forward, a front head butt or inward hammerfist strike can use that increased forward acceleration to strike an attacker's face (Fist of Aggression).

Example: Pulling – As one of our shoulders is pulled from behind, causing us to step back and turn, adds accumulative force to our 180º of rotational energy as we turn, drop to a close kneel stance, and punch him in the lower abdomen or groin (Ducking Dragon).

Example: Pulling - As one of our shoulders is pulled from behind, causing us to step back and turn, adding to our torsos 180º of rotational energy as we turn with a handsword strike directly into the attacker's throat (Hidden Hand).

Example: Pushing - An opponent's right hand pushes our left shoulder from the front, i.e. straight push, thereby accelerating our right shoulder forward using the *Force Couple* principle thereby speeding up our straight palm strike into his chin/face (Triggered Palm).

Example: Pushing - An opponent's right hand pushes our right shoulder from in front, i.e. cross push, thereby accelerating our left shoulder forward using the *Force Couple* principle against his elbow joint as our other hand traps his wrist in the opposite direction to scissor that elbow joint (Glancing Palm).

VOLUNTARY MOMENTUM

Whenever we choose to put our body in motion this momentum of mass is generated. It defines using our own structure with singular motions or compounding body parts that start with the momentum of one motion to help with the momentum of another. Moving a singular part like lifting the bent knee to strike and/or then extending the lower leg to execute a kick with the foot is a simple type of example (Thrusting Palm) used throughout martial arts.

Note: It's important to understand that even though we consciously put our own weapons in motion with intention and acceleration they still have their own weight and momentum that apply their own mass. This adds inertia to any force being applied while using our natural weapons and should be encouraged to occur, like how a stick or knife is used as a weapon.

Although *Voluntary Momentum* is most obviously used by us against an opponent, we can also use their *Voluntary Momentum* against them. This uses intended and unintended weapons or obstacles with the momentum and inertia that accompanies someone else's intended aggressive motion. It takes advantage of another person's momentum without their permission by either *interrupting their initiated action*, by *moving the intended target*, or as a natural and perhaps unintentional *defensive reaction* to an attack by us or them. Whatever the use, it is a real force that we should understand and utilize.

Examples: Interrupting their Initiated Action Voluntary Momentum – An opponent charging forward runs into your extending side kick (Purple Belt Sparring #6); attacker lunging forward with an overhead strike runs his armpit into an extended forward elbow tip (Protective Circles); opponent aggressively lunging forward to tackle adds weight and acceleration into extended palms striking his collarbones (Jamming Tackle).

Examples: Moving the Intended Target or Obstacle Voluntary Momentum – An opponent aggressively lunging forward to tackle meets empty space after we side step, and perhaps guide, them into a wall behind us and/or we hit them down to the ground (Charging Tackle); attacker lunging with a punch meets air as we step offline allowing them or guiding them into an obstacle or follow-up strikes (Reversing Fist).

Examples: Opponents Unintended Reaction Voluntary Momentum – Stepping offline against forward (Twin Lapel Grab) or rear (Circling Elbow) pushing pressure causes an opponent's energy to move past us into a more vulnerable and unbalanced position where they are countered.

Examples: Our Unintended Reaction Voluntary Momentum – In jumping back to avoid a takedown attempt, our head lunges forward striking them in the face with a head butt; we extend our arms while defending their tackle attempt unintentionally poking them in the eyes with our fingers. Both of these can be seen on occasion in sport fighting.

MANIPULATED VOLUNTARY MOMENTUM

Stress caused at a joint by applying pressure, perhaps forceful and extreme, that causes a physical voluntary movement adjustment in a different direction then originally intended by an attacker. To relieve pressure an opponent is encouraged to unwittingly change direction moving towards a place not intended by them.

This is then utilized to guide them into a position for control and follow-up techniques, or another position change is inserted making for a follow-up redirection to cause more damage to unprepared body parts.

Examples: Manipulating the Wrist, Elbow, and Shoulder – Rotating around their hand and outside wrist to help cancel and manipulate (Crossing Grab); rotating around their hand and inside wrist to line their elbow over our shoulder to damage and move their body mass from the pressure (Entangled Arm A); twisting the hand while pushing the bent elbow to rotate the shoulder joint causing their body mass to turn over (Piercing Blade); an outward wrist lock moves an attacker in one direction where a sudden direction change is then applied using an inward wrist lock to manipulate in the opposite direction, possibly causing wrist and/or arm damage (Reversing Circles).

Examples: Manipulating the Torso – Moving an attacker's body mass by pushing, lifting then turning their head and body around and off balance before driving their head/neck onto the ground (Crossed Arms); moving backwards against a low tackle while striking and pushing down on their back with continuous manipulative downward striking momentum driving them towards the ground (Meeting the Tackle).

Examples: Manipulating the Ankle, Knee, and Hip – Twisting the ankle to turn an opponent over (Dance of Death); sitting onto a rear attacker's knee while pulling their foot forward (Straddling the Leg); pushing the hip while lifting their foot with an ankle pick to drive them onto their back on the ground (The Nutcracker).

INVOLUNTARY MOMENTUM

When a part or an entire body is forced, directed, or tricked into moving in open space, or into a natural weapon (e.g., foot or hand), or an inanimate surface (e.g., floor, wall, boxing ring ropes, MMA cage, etc.), by *Pushing*, *Pulling* or as a *Reflex Response*.

Note: *Pushing* or *Pulling* can be followed by *Pressing* to maintain control once movement space is eliminated. These are all used to maintain/create/eliminate space, control, setup, neutralize (check), break balance, cause pain, and/or affect a release from a grip or hold.

All three can be seen in a wrestling or Judo clinch where a push causes a reaction that sets up a pull, and vice-versa. This is used with timing to setup and take advantage of this momentary vulnerability. Strikers create this in open space with fakes, feints, traps, etc.

Pushing is an accelerated motion that starts with space between the contact points after making a surface connection through *impact* or after *attaching* as in grappling. A completed push can then be released to create space for striking or stick to the target and continue pushing, perhaps into another surface where pushing then becomes pressing.

Example: Torso Pushing – While leaning against each other a boxer can use his shoulder to push (bump) an opponent's upper torso to create space. This space often allows for an uppercut punch to lift under the chin or for footwork to be inserted allowing for angle and distance adjustments.

Example: Arm Pushing – An upward rolling forearm under an attacker's chin can shift his weight to his heels chin while holding his head up exposing his throat to a strike (Pursuing Panther).

Examples: Pressing – Holding an opponent with pressure against a wall using a cross-body shoulder check (Bouncing Pendulum); a horizontal forearm pressed against an opponent's throat pushing and holding them against a wall, possibly crushing their windpipe (Taming the Fist).

Pulling requires holding or hooking part of an attacker's body often at the wrists or neck to either bring them closer to us, to the ground, or into an object. It can also be combined with other body area manipulations like sweeps to assist in the pull being more successful.

Example: Pulling in Space – Counter-grabbing a double wrist grab then pulling the attacker forward onto their toes into a front groin kick, then follow-up strikes (Begging Palms).

Examples: Pulling after Pushing – After jamming an attempted tackle (pushing) then pull or jerk them down to the ground after feeling resistance (Jamming the Tackle); pushing a forward elbow strike into their collarbone then pulling forward and down (Detouring the Kick).

Example: Pulling Down after Sweep Assist – Securing an attacker's neck to pull their head down into a knee kick after widening their base with a sweep (Sweeping the Leg)

Example: Pulling to Stack Opponents – After striking and tenderizing two attackers, one is pulled down to the ground then the other is stacked on top of him pressing one onto the other (Flowing Hands).

Reflex Response is a body reaction caused by a sense of vulnerability, or contact causing a neuromuscular reflex and/or a change in posture from reaction to a sensitive area being attacked, all causing an alternate target/weapon to accelerate. This awareness is also important for checking our own potential targets.

Example: Neuromuscular Response – Hammering the bicep, causing the muscle to violently contract (i.e., Muscle Spindle Cell-MSC Reflex), combined with a checked wrist causes their elbow to move away opening their neck for a handsword strike (Six Hands); rubbing the base of the tricep muscle causing the elbow to lock straight into hyper-extension (i.e., Golgi Tendon Organ-GTO Reflex), used for body manipulation and to possibly injure (Obstructing the Club).

Example: Sensitive Area Response – Front kicking the groin causes the head to come forward into a straight palm strike (Thrusting Palm). Three different timing components that exist in this technique can take to advantage of this response.

Timing #1: Hitting the palm strike *as* our foot settles on the ground (i.e., marriage of gravity), and is how the base technique is designed. This powerful method gives the attacker time to bend forward which can provide alternate head targets. However, an experienced and/or athletic attacker would have more time to see and adjust to this timing.

Timing #2: The palm strike happens after the groin kick but *before* our foot settles onto the floor, a staggered beat timing. This most likely has less power than Timing #1 but since it gives the attacker less adjustment time that could be made up by the target vulnerability factor, and it would tend to keep him more upright. Another benefit is that as the foot settles a secondary strike can be added like a forward vertical elbow to sternum strike.

Timing #3: The groin kick and palm strike happen *simultaneously*, also allowing for another follow up as the weight settles. The vertical horseshoe punch also applies this dual strike method (Twins of Destruction).

Defensively, it is important that we protect ourselves from this reflexive response as it could result from something we did to an opponent. This is done using *Checking*.

Examples: Need for Checking – Kneeing an opponent's groin in defense from a front bear hug (Thrusting Thumbs) may cause his head to lunge forward striking us in the face; or elbowing his chin (Destructive Gift) may cause his front leg to intentionally or unintentionally lift into our groin.

BIBLIOGRAPHY

Deadman, Peter. <u>A Manual of Acupuncture</u>. 1998 Journal of Medicine Publications, 22 Cromwell Rd Hove East Sussex BN3 3EB England

Parker, Edmund K. <u>Infinite Insights into Kenpo Series 1-5</u>. 1982 Delsby Publications, Pasadena California

Parker, Edmund K. <u>Encyclopedia of Kenpo</u>. 1992 Delsby Publications, Pasadena California

Liu, Sing-Han. Ba Gua: Hidden Knowledge in the Taoist Internal Martial Art. 1998 Liu Sing-Han and Bracy, John Publishing

Adams, Brian. The Medical Implications of Karate Blows. Published 1969

Howstuffworks.com
Nutritiondata.com
Webmd.com
Mathisfun.com
Molossia.org
Wingchunonline.com
Scientificpsychic.com
Nlh.nih.gov/medlineplus
Pitt.edu
Mediral.com
Your-doctor.com
Scribd.com

ABOUT THE AUTHOR

Barry B Barker (aka Mr. B) is a father of 5 kids, with 6 grandkids, and 87 Black Belts as of this 2021 4th Edition (See Black Belt Family Tree in 'Spirit'). Mr. B is a 9th Degree Kenpo Black Belt in his American Kenpo Alliance (AKA) Kenpo system having been a full-time school owner and teacher for over 35 years while running Poway Kenpo Karate/Poway Martial Arts, which he founded in 1984. He is also a Licensed Acupuncturist, Author, BarryBBarker.com owner, and a competitive Salsa Dancer.

Mr. B became interested in martial arts after watching Bruce Lee as a child. He first enrolled in martial arts at Brian Adams Kenpo Karate School in San Diego, California in 1973 for a brief time, Parker Linekin was his instructor.

He dabbled in various martial arts styles until 1980 when he found an Ed Parker Kenpo Karate School located in El Cajon, California. That school was run by a very technical instructor, and private student of Mr. Parker, Jim Mitchell (does the stance work photos in Mr. Parker's Book #2). Mr. Barker earned his 1st Degree Black Belt at this school in 1983, with Mr. Parker as a member of his testing board.

In 1984, Jim Mitchell promoted Mr. Barker to 2nd Degree Black Belt and in the same year Mr. B opened Aaction Kenpo Karate, as a Jim Mitchell affiliate school, then later changed that to Poway Kenpo Karate.

He was promoted to 3rd Degree in 1987 then 4th Degree in 1990. Mr. Mitchell moved out of state shortly thereafter, so Mr. B formed his own American Kenpo Alliance (AKA) martial art association in 1992 to administer to his own Kenpo students.

Additional certification came in 1994 by Orned "Chicken" Gabriel and Steve "Nasty" Anderson, recognizing Mr. Barker as a 4th Degree in their United Karate Federation (UKF). IKKA Master Instructor Ernest George Jr. promoted Mr. Barker to 5th Degree in 1995 then 6th Degree in 2000.

Mr. Barker expanded his training facility in 1998 when he opened a Muay Thai gym called World Class Kickboxing, later becoming The Boxing Club. He added Brazilian Jiu Jitsu in 2005 and MMA in 2008. All of that became part of what is now known as Poway Martial Arts.

He was promoted to 7th Degree in 2005 by Rick Hughes and Willy Steele, both Ed Parker Black Belts and IKKA Master Instructors'. In 2010 he was promoted to 8th Degree by GM Parker Linekin, with additional authorization provided from SGM Brian Adams and in 2015 to 9th Degree as authorized by SGM Brian Adams, GM Parker Linekin, GM Orned "Chicken" Gabriel, and GM Reynaldo Leal.

In addition to running Poway Kenpo Karate and Poway Martial Arts, Mr. Barker pursued his education and graduated from Pacific College of Oriental Medicine with a Master's in Traditional Oriental Medicine (MSTOM) in 2007. He is a Nationally Certified (Dipl. O.M.) and a California Acupuncturist (L.Ac.).

This Mind-Body-Spirit book series is a project he gave himself to further his personal growth and contribute to his family, students, and the martial art community.

Mr. Barker has turned daily operations of Poway Kenpo Karate and Poway Martial Arts over to his children for them to continue the family legacy. He still teaches seminars/workshops and treats his Acupuncture patients and manages his Kenpo video site BarryBBarker.com where his entire Kenpo System is available to see and learn. In 2014, his school celebrated 30 years in business, then 36 years in 2020, and the school he founded is highly regarded in the local community.

As an avid learner and student of martial arts, Mr. Barker has also sought additional training over the years to continue and enhance his own skills.

Additional training:
Ed Parker, Advanced Kenpo Theory • Jeff Speakman, Kenpo Seminar • Joe Lewis, several Fight Training Seminars • Steve Nasty Anderson, several Fight Training Seminars • Orned Chicken Gabriel, 2 Years Personal Training & many Fight Training Seminars • Brian Adams, Knife & Stick Fighting Seminar • Dave Hebler, Power & Speed Seminar • Richard Post, Knife Fighting Seminar • Rick Hughes, many Classes & Seminars • Willy Steele, many Classes & Seminars • Toke Hill, Olympic Style Sparring Seminar • Mike Stone, Martial Arts Seminars • Eric Lee, Martial Arts Training Seminar • Parker Linekin, many years of Seminars & Training • John Denora, Daito Ryu Seminar • George Dillman, Pressure Point Seminar • Prof. Wally Jay, several Small Circle Jiu Jitsu Seminars • Royce Gracie, Brazilian Jiu Jitsu Seminars • Nelson Monteiro, Brazilian Jiu Jitsu 2 Years Training & Seminars • Carlos Valente, Brazilian Jiu Jitsu 1 Year Training and Seminars • Vic Zamora, Boxing Personal Training • Vincent Soberano, Muay Thai Personal Training • Melchor Menor, Muay Thai Seminars & Classes • Nelson Siyavong, several Muay Thai Seminars • Kaewsamrit Muay Thai Training Camp, 2 Weeks Bangkok Thailand • Cepeda Brothers, Arnis de Mano Classes • Krav Maga, Certification Seminar • CDT, Certification Seminar • Cung Lee, San Shou Seminar • Jim Tian, Tai Chi Chuan several years • Frank Primicias, Lo Han Chi Gung Seminars • Chen Sitan, Taiji Seminar • Rey Leal, Tai Chi Personal Training • International Training Program, Chengdu University of Chinese Medicine in Chengdu, China

Mr. Barker has also been recognized more formally in other ways. Some of those recognitions are listed below:

- Inducted Golden Global Martial Arts Hall of Fame 1998
- Inducted Masters Hall of Fame 2000
- Inducted World Amateur Martial Arts International Federation 2006
- Listed Heritage Registry of Who's Who 2007
- City of Poway Mayors Commendation for Civic Work 2010 & 2014
- CA State Senate Community Service Commendation 2012, 2014, 2017
- Inducted USA Martial Arts Hall of Fame 2014
- Presidential Fitness Award 2017

Made in the USA
Columbia, SC
22 June 2022